Celebrate the Seasons!

With The Dunwoody Gourmet Group

Contributors

Cookbook Chairman
Joan "Queenie" Ross

Recipe Development
Pat Coker
Sue Keenan
Sandy Kirkley
Gloria Lee
Ginger Paul
Queenie Ross
Clare Schelhammer
Barbara Washington

Editors
Sue Keenan
Clare Schelhammer
Ginger Paul
Queenie Ross

Tablescape Design and Photography
Gloria Lee
Barbara Washington

Professional Credits

Typesetting and Computer Consultant
TC Ryker

Cover and Artistic Layout
Lucian Kapuscinski - Kap & Company

*We are grateful to our friends and family who have
given us encouragement and support, and
to our spouses and children, thank you for your patience and enthusiasm.
A special thanks to Danny Ross for making the production of this book possible.*

Copyright 1996

Please note that the quantities given in all recipes
serve 12 people unless otherwise stated.

Library of Congress catalog number:
96-61390

ISBN 1-883793-21-1

Additional copies of **Celebrate The Seasons** may be obtained by writing
The Dunwoody Gourmet Group
2482 Jett Ferry Road, #680 D21
Atlanta, Georgia 30338 USA

or call toll free 1-800-768-9346.

Published in Atlanta, Georgia, USA 1996

OUR STORY

The idea of our Gourmet Group evolved in late 1976 in Dunwoody, a suburb of Atlanta, Georgia. Six couples who shared an appreciation for dining and entertaining were drawn together. They comprised an interesting mix of personalities and talents. We fondly recall that first meal with the French theme and the menu of Escargot, Vichyssoise, Coq-au-Vin and Roulage Chocolat. The evening was a huge success but we had exhausted everything we knew of gourmet, so the question loomed, "What next?" The answer has been a gastronomic adventure that spans not only growth in the exploration of fine foods, but a sharing of our families and lives to produce lasting friendships.

Through the years, our approach to cooking has become less complicated, though no less gourmet, and there is always room for creativity. We increasingly take advantage of the wonderful new foods available at the local and international farmers' markets. Fresh herbs collected from our gardens or from the market are lavishly used for flavor or for garnishing.

January marks the time when the eight ladies convene, calendars in hand, to plan the year's six dinner celebrations. This gathering and the menu planning sessions before each dinner have become a very special part of our Gourmet Group process and often extend into the wee hours. Concocting an evening's repast is a collaborative effort throughout which books are consulted, wine is enjoyed and the ideas abound. The result is an evening of camaraderie that always yields a winning menu.

Careful planning lends itself to creating that special evening when the couples in our group gather to share the delicious meal presented graciously at a host home. Most often, the host husband will act as wine steward and several of the husbands are proficient carvers. As our greatest supporters, our spouses eat and enjoy everything we cook, occasionally lobbying for the main course to contain beef, fish or more beef! Their principal role though is to praise, praise, praise!

Travel has become a particular focus of the members of this group. A trip to the south of France and Italy was the perfect way to celebrate our Twentieth Anniversary of gourmet dining together and to enjoy many of the international foods that we have learned to prepare.

Many people have been curious about our Gourmet Group and have encouraged us to reveal our recipes. Thus was born the idea for this cookbook, *Celebrate The Seasons*, which contains twenty menus for **twelve,** spanning five seasons, our fifth season being "Holiday."

The first French meal that was prepared by our Dunwoody Gourmet Group was successful enough to inspire the question, "What next?" Twenty years of friendship and creative dining have been the dynamic response to that question in a way that is truly a "celebration."

Come *Celebrate The Seasons* with us!

TABLE OF CONTENTS

STARTING YOUR OWN GOURMET GROUP

SUGGESTIONS:

- The size of the group is the first determining factor when organizing your gourmet group. Four, five or six couples is the usual number. This is based on the size of your dining rooms and how many settings of china and silver each person owns.

- Choose friends that are compatible, enjoy cooking and experimenting with new cuisines, or are willing to learn.

- Establish your dates by meeting with your calendars in hand. Hosting one dinner per year per couple is usually advisable, considering busy work and travel schedules.

- Discuss in advance how the group will share the expenses. We suggest keeping records of the providers of each course and assigning it fairly each time. Costs will usually equalize. Or you might divide the cost of each dinner between each couple.

- To begin, the hostess calls a meeting a week or so before the scheduled date to plan the menu and assign each course. Choose one of the menus in *Celebrate The Seasons* or create your own gourmet delight. If a theme is chosen, that is usually determined by the host couple.

- Consider hiring help to serve and clean up the kitchen. It is a great feeling to bid "good night" to your guests and walk back into a tidy kitchen. (Our group trained their sons and daughters to do this over the years. Some have grown up to be "gourmets" also.)

- Cocktails, wine and flowers are usually the responsibility of the host couple. When assigning their course, we suggest allowing them to choose one that is not as time consuming, such as soup or salad.

- Write out your recipe and give to the hostess who will distribute complete menus to all of your group for future reference.

- Relax and enjoy the evening. Hopefully, you will be sharing these wonderful meals with your friends for many years to come.

ENTERTAINING CHECKLIST

Decide on menu
Plan table setting, linens, dishes, etc.
Plan centerpiece
Prepare food which can be made ahead
Purchase wine
Check bar supplies
Hire kitchen help

DINNER IS SERVED

Although the trend of the day is away from the formal dinner and toward informal or casual dining, we would like to offer our suggestions for keeping your party FORMAL but FUN.

Setting a beautiful table can be easy. When entertaining guests in your dining room, just follow the guide below eliminating any pieces that won't be needed. Color and warmth can be added with attractive linens. White damask or lace is the most formal but colored linen coordinating with your china can be beautiful. Emily Post's rule for lighting is one candle for every two settings, which translates to three pair for a table of twelve. Placecards are a must to avoid confusion when being seated for dinner. Napkins can either be placed on top of the dinner plate folded in a decorative way or to the left of the dinner plate (see table suggestions accompanying each menu). Dinner plate and charger (optional) are arranged one inch from the edge of the table. The flatware is arranged with knife (blade turned toward plate) and spoons on the right and forks on the left, except for cocktail forks which are placed to the right of the soup spoon. Dessert forks or spoons are placed above the plate as indicated by the guide. The water glass is placed above the knife and the wine glass to the right of the water glass. Soup and salad are usually served as a separate course and placed on top of the dinner plate or charger. Bread and butter plates are optional, depending on the table room. Coffee and dessert plates are usually stored until the course is served.

WINTER MENUS

ROSES AND CANDLELIGHT

Bacon and Tomato Baskets

Caviar Salmon Crêpes with Crème Frâiche

Love-A-Pepper Soup

Garlic and Parmesan Toasts

Organic Mixed Greens with
Honey Lemon Vinaigrette

Pork Medallions with
Pears and Camembert

Rice Pilaf with Pistachios
and Pine Nuts

Sautéed Sugar Snaps

Strawberry Sweetheart Meringue Cake

MARDI GRAS SEAFOOD EXTRAVAGANZA

Oysters Washington

Sautéed Crawfish on Mixed Greens
With Creole Andouille Sauce

Queenie's Imperial Crab Gumbo

Pompano on Parade

Broiled Tomato Halves
with Herbs and Gruyére

Braised Celery with Toasted Almonds

Apple Bread Pudding Soufflé
with Whiskey Sauce

King Cake

Le Café

RAINY NIGHT IN LONDON

Mushroom Terrine

Artichokes Alistair

Oyster and Spinach Cream Soup

Watercress and Grape Salad with
Toasted Nuts and Lemon Cream Dressing

Sautéed Veal Chops
with Stilton and Currant Sauce

Fanned New Potatoes and Fresh Tarragon

English Peas in Radicchio Cups

Derbyshire Bakewell Tart

A FIRESIDE AFFAIR

Warmed Herb Cheese Spread

Sherried Mushroom Strudel

Corn and Crab Bisque

Mixed Winter Greens
with Chutney Dijon Dressing

Roast Duckling with Blackberry Sauce

Carrot Soufflé

Braised Brussels Sprouts
with Chestnuts and Shallots

Walnut Crème Gâteau

SPRING MENUS

GOURMET IN BLOOM

Roasted Elephant Garlic Flowerette

Mussel Velouté with Saffron and Fennel

Spring Asparagus Salad

Sherried Tenderloin of Beef
with Currants and Green Peppercorn
Sauce

Tarragon Carrots by Crispin

Rosemary New Potatoes

Almond Frangelico Ice Cream Torte

APRIL IN PARIS

Petite Pinwheels

Coquille St. Jacques avec Champignon

Brie Bisque

Evantail Française

Sea Bass En Croûte with Shallot
Hollandaise

Haricots Verts

Crêpes De Fraises Royale

HAPPINESS IS...SPRING FEVER

Walnut Camembert Paté

Drunken Prawns

Caramelized Vidalia Onion Soup
with Roasted Shallots

Romaine and Pepper Medley with
Cashews

Spring Gourmet Lamb Chops

Porcini Mushroom Risotto

Roasted Asparagus
with Grapefruit Hollandaise

Spring Fruit Trifle

BUDDHA'S BIRTHDAY FEAST

Beef and Pork Satays with Peanut Sauce

Pattaya Scallops

Hot and Sour Prawn Soup

Green Papaya in Tomato Flower

Gaeng Kiow Wahn Gai

Thai Fried Noodles

"Som" Celebration Cups
with Cointreau Sauce

Buddha's Lace Fans

SUMMER MENUS

CITY SLICKERS GO WEST

Glen's Margaritas

Spicy Salsa with Blue Corn Chips

Stuffed Poblano with Shrimp and Chèvre

Avocado Soup Teased with Tequila

Cactus Salad

Tombstone Tuna with Mango Relish

Santa Fe Saffron Rice

Coco Loco Flan

Skewered Fruit

SUMMERTIME . . . WHEN THE COOKIN' IS EASY

Mozzarella and Garlic Bruschetta

Soft Shell Crabs Amandine

Chilled Asparagus Cream Soup

Tomato Basil Salad with Feta Cheese

Aw Shucks Salmon

Au Gratin Potatoes with Peppered Boursin

Lemon Chiffon Mousse with Walnut Date Crust

GEORGIA ON MY MIND

Angel Biscuits with Country Ham and Apple Butter

Fried Green Tomatoes with Crab and Parsley-Basil Pesto

Savannah Seafood Chowder

Red Cabbage, Apple and Roquefort Slaw

Peachy Chicken with Brandy Cream Sauce

Crispy Baked Mashed Potatoes

Bronzed Spinach with Mushrooms

Chocolate Peanut Chiffon Pie

"SIMPLY" ELEGANT

Pass-The-Ratatouille

Gusto Shrimp Gazpacho

Baby Spinach Salad with Grilled Onions and Gorgonzola

Grilled Steaks with Bourbon Sauce

Mushroom Cheese Grits

Steamed Broccoli with Horseradish Cream

Berry Peachy Pockets

HARVEST MENUS

AFTER THE HUNT

Hot Sausage Packages

Sautéed Portabello Mushrooms with Mussels

Pumpkin Soup in a Pumpkin

Pears and Walnuts over Chilled Greens "A La Daniel"

Quail with Apple Brandy Cream Sauce

Couscous with Sautéed Vegetables

Chocolate Pecan Bourbon Cake with Bittersweet Glaze and Raspberry Coulis

HARVEST CELEBRATION

Bayou Crawfish Mousse

Pasta Gloria

Cream of Apple Soup with Campazola Croûtons

Arugula and Crab Salad with Warm Sherry Vinaigrette

Rolled Loin of Pork Stuffed with Apricots and Pistachios

Soufflé of Sweet Potatoes and Gruyère

Zucchini Cups with Buttered Peas and Baby Squash

Pear William Puffs with Créme Anglaise

FIESTA CON AMIGOS EN ESPAÑA

Tapas

Empañadas Con Carne De Cordero

Champiñones al Ajillo

Sopa De Calabaza y Ajo

Ensalada De Los Moros

Cocino Asado

Arroz Primavera Con Azafran

Tarta De Los Musicianos

Cafe Español

PRELUDE TO THE OPERA

Antipasto

Crostini Alle Olive

Proscuitto E Melone

Mellanzane Alla Mozzarella

Pepperoni Alle Acciughe

"Zuppa" of Leek and Portabella Mushrooms

Insalata Di Fagioli and Salsiccia

Tomato Pesto Linquine Topped with Fried Calamari

Tiramisu Soufflé

Figs with Almond Mascarpone Filling

Caffè Romano Caldo

HOLIDAY MENUS

'TIS THE SEASON ...

Brie with Sun Dried Tomatoes

Shrimp and Saga on Crostini

Fresh Mushroom Vermouth Soup

Pomegranate and Spinach Salad with
Warm Champagne Dressing

Holiday Stuffed Beef Tenderloin

Duchess Potato Rings with Bronzed
Carrots

Sautéed Snow Peas and Cherry Tomatoes

White Chocolate Mousse Cake with
Cranberries Jubilee

CHAMPAGNE AND CAVIAR CHRISTMAS

Elegant Caviar Tarte

Champagne Oysters and Shrimp

Roasted Chestnut Bisque

Chilled Romaine with Hot Brie Dressing

Fruit Filled Christmas Goose

Wild Rice with Sausage and Prunes

Green Bean Bundles

Cappucino Fantasy

SLEIGH BELLS AND STRUDEL

Prosciutto Wrapped Asparagus

Duck Breasts with Brandied Cherry Sauce

Sherried Pistachio Soup

Festive Greens with Cranberry Vinaigrette

Seafood Strudel

Lemon Rice Pilaf

Spinach Stuffed Plum Tomato

Gâteau Nègre Praliné

AN ATLANTA CHRISTMAS

Shrimp Stuffed New Potatoes

Nutcracker Fettucini

Orange Carrot Soup

Lobster and Asparagus Salad

Peppercorn Crusted Roast Pork
with Brandy Sauce

Cranberry Chutney

Seasonal Sage Stuffing

Petite Choco-mint Soufflés with
Crème de Menthe Sauce

Winter

ROSES AND CANDLELIGHT

Bacon and Tomato Baskets

Caviar Salmon Crêpes with Crème Frâiche

Love-a-Pepper Soup

Garlic and Parmesan Toasts

Organic Mixed Greens with Honey Lemon Vinaigrette

Pork Medallions with Pears and Camembert

Rice Pilaf with Pistachios and Pine Nuts

Sautéed Sugar Snaps

Strawberry Sweetheart Meringue Cake

SERVES 12

What could be more romantic

than a candlelight dinner on a cold winter night?

Dining has always been a ceremonious occasion

and needs a romantic ambience.

The table setting with its fine china and sparkling glass,

a wonderful centerpiece, the flattering flicker of candlelight,

all play a part in creating an event to remember.

Cut-glass crystal rose bowls filled with pink roses and

numerous candlesticks of different heights will add warmth.

Scatter additional rose petals on the table.

The fragrance of the roses will fill your evening.

Candlelight is warm and flattering, make it a part of all your dinners.

Lay a single rose across each plate and tie with a ribbon...

an elegant touch for a special menu.

Maintain the romantic mood through the dinner

by playing the music of Mozart.

Bacon and Tomato Baskets

2 packages frozen mini-phyllo dough shells or 1 package puff pastry
8 slices bacon, fried crisp, drained and crumbled
1 medium tomato, seeded and chopped
1/2 small onion, excess moisture removed
3/4 cup shredded Jarlsberg cheese (about 3 ounces)
1/3 cup mayonnaise
1 tablespoon fresh basil.

If using puff pastry, roll out on a lightly floured surface and cut circles to fit miniature muffin pans. Lightly grease pan, if not using teflon. Combine bacon, tomato, onion, cheese, mayonnaise, basil and mix well. Drop bacon mixture by teaspoons into muffin cups. Bake in preheated 375° oven for 8 minutes. If using phyllo shells, bake 12 to 15 minutes.

Caviar Salmon Crêpes with Crème Frâiche

Crêpes
1-1/2 cups milk
1-1/2 cups plain flour
4 eggs
2 tablespoons fresh dill
4 tablespoons butter, melted
1-1/2 pounds smoked salmon, thinly sliced
2 cups crème frâiche or sour cream
8 ounces caviar, red, yellow, black, or a combination
Fresh dill for garnish

Crème Frâiche
2 cups heavy cream, not ultra-pasteurized
4 tablespoons buttermilk

To prepare Crème Frâiche: Several days ahead, combine cream with buttermilk, mixing well. Cover lightly with plastic wrap. Do not seal. Leave at room temperature for 12 to 24 hours. It will begin to thicken at this time. Then cover well and keep refrigerated until serving time. It will keep for up to 5 days in the refrigerator. (At serving time, if crème frâiche is too thin, add sour cream to thicken.)

For Crêpes: Combine the milk, flour, eggs and dill and mix well with an electric mixer. Add melted butter and mix well, scraping down sides of bowl. Let stand 30 minutes. Brush a small (8 inch) crêpe pan with butter. When pan is very hot, pour in enough batter (approximately 1/8 cup) to cover the bottom of the pan. The crêpe should be very thin. You may need to tilt and rotate the pan to make the crêpe uniform. When crêpe is

"Love is a flame that must constantly be re-kindled to keep from diminishing."

Author unknown

We know a burning candle sheds more than mere light. It reminds us of the warmth we feel tonight.

Always make a little bit extra so that the kitchen help can have a sample. We always hire our teenage children to help with our dinners. Many are gourmet cooks in their own right today!

*This is a uniquely
colorful soup and
will surely evoke
praise!*

lightly browned around the edges, flip carefully, brown slightly and then turn it onto a piece of waxed paper. Cover with another piece of paper and continue with the remaining batter. Makes 18 6-inch crêpes. (Any extra crêpes may be frozen in a plastic bag, each separated by a sheet of waxed paper.)

With crêpes at room temperature, put a generous slice of smoked salmon on top of each crêpe. Put a tablespoon of crème frâiche on top of salmon. Fold crêpe in half or roll it. Put a generous spoonful of crème frâiche or sour cream on top. Garnish with a teaspoon of caviar, or a bit of two or three colors of caviar. Top with a sprig of dill and serve.

Love-A-Pepper Soup

6 red bell peppers
6 yellow bell peppers
2 tablespoons olive oil
3-1/2 cups chopped onion
2 cups diced carrots
1 cup diced celery
12 cups chicken stock
4 medium potatoes, peeled and diced
2 bay leaves
1/4 teaspoon cayenne pepper
1 teaspoon ground cumin
1 teaspoon ground coriander
Salt and pepper to taste
Parsley

Broil peppers in broiler or on a gas grill until blackened on all sides, turning frequently. Place peppers in a closed plastic or paper bag for 15 minutes. Peel all blackened skin under running water. Discard stem and seeds. Keep red and yellow peppers separated. (Can be prepared two days ahead.)

Sauté onions, carrots and celery in the olive oil until tender (about 10 minutes). Add stock, potatoes, cayenne pepper and bay leaves. Cover and simmer 30 minutes until potatoes are very tender. Remove bay leaves, divide soup in half. Add yellow peppers to one half, and red peppers to the other half. Puree each mixture separately and return to separate sauce pans. Stir cumin into red pepper soup, and coriander into yellow soup. Salt and pepper to taste. Ladle each soup at same time, side by side, into the bowls. Garnish with parsley. Makes 2-1/2 to 3 quarts.

Serve with Garlic and Parmesan Toasts (recipe follows on page 8).

Garlic and Parmesan Toasts

— • ○ ● • —

24 1/2-inch thick sliced French baguette
1 tablespoon olive oil
6 garlic cloves, finely chopped
1/4 cup grated Parmesan cheese
1 teaspoon oregano
1/4 teaspoon pepper

Preheat oven to 350°. Sauté garlic in olive oil until golden (about 2 minutes). Drain garlic and discard oil. Combine garlic, cheese, oregano and pepper. Sprinkle over bread slices. Bake for about 10 minutes, until cheese melts and toasts have golden edges. Pass separately with the soup.

Organic Mixed Greens with Honey Lemon Vinaigrette

— • ○ ● • —

3 tablespoons honey
3 tablespoons vinegar
1/3 cup mayonnaise
1-1/4 tablespoons Dijon mustard
1 tablespoon lemon juice
1-1/2 tablespoons finely minced green onions
1-1/2 tablespoons chopped fresh parsley
Pinch of salt
1 tablespoon water
3/4 to 1 cup vegetable oil
12 cups mixed organic greens (examples: arugula, endive, romaine and bibb lettuce)
12 kumquats or 12 red or yellow pepper rings

Heat honey and vinegar over low heat for one minute until honey dissolves. Cool in bowl. Whisk in mayonnaise, mustard, onions, lemon juice, parsley, water and salt. Gradually whisk in oil. (Can be prepared 2 days ahead.) Cover and refrigerate. Set out 30 minutes before serving.

Arrange greens on salad plates and drizzle dressing individually over each plate. Garnish with kumquats or red or yellow pepper rings.

You may choose to serve a simple salad after the entree as done in many European countries.

Types of salad greens: When choosing salad greens, experiment with the expanded selection of colors and textures that are now available. Mix a delicate bibb or Boston with a peppery arugula or combine romaine with a curly Belgian endive. Create one that's perfect for your taste.

Pork Medallions with Pears and Camembert

3 whole pork tenderloins (approximately 1-1/2 pounds each), cut in half,
    6 pieces total
2 pears (any variety) sliced
1 pound Camembert cheese (2 8-ounce rounds)
4-1/2 tablespoons unsalted butter
1 tablespoon olive oil
Celebration Seasoning *
Fresh tarragon leaves for garnish

Demi-glace
4 slices bacon
1 onion, chopped
1 carrot, finely chopped
1 celery stalk, finely chopped
1/3 cup flour
1/3 cup unsalted butter
6 cups beef stock or broth
1 teaspoon fresh thyme
1 bay leaf
1/4 cup tomato paste
1/4 cup dry white wine

Season tenderloins with Celebration Seasoning. Sauté 3 tablespoons of butter and 1 tablespoon of olive oil in heavy skillet for approximately 10 minutes to seal in juices. Set aside.

Demi-glace: Fry bacon, drain and crumble. Sauté onion, carrot and celery in bacon drippings 8 to 10 minutes. Drain. In saucepan melt butter. Blend in flour and cook until lightly browned. Blend in 4 cups broth, saving 2 cups, stirring until slightly thickened. Add bacon, vegetables, thyme and bay leaf. Boil, uncovered for 30 minutes. Strain well, add 1/4 cup tomato paste and simmer for another 20 minutes. Add 1 cup beef stock and boil until reduced to 3 cups. Stir in 1/4 cup dry white wine. Place meat in large baking pan. Pour 1 cup broth over meat and bake in 400° oven for approximately 20 minutes, or until meat thermometer registers 155° to 160°.

In the meantime, melt 1-1/2 tablespoons butter in skillet and sauté pear slices for 1 to 2 minutes. Cut Camembert cheese in 12 slices. Slice pork into 1 inch medallions.

Place on an oven proof platter. Put slice of pear, then slice of Camembert on top of each medallion. Heat a few minutes at 350° until cheese is melted.

Ladle demi-glace on each dinner plate. Place medallions on top. Garnish with fresh tarragon leaves.

* See recipe for Celebration Seasoning, page 14 side note.

Rice Pilaf with Pistachios and Pine Nuts

▪••●••▪

6 cups chicken stock
3 cups long grain white rice

1/4 cup butter
1 cup pine nuts
1 cup unsalted shelled pistachios
1 teaspoon salt
1 teaspoon nutmeg
Salt and pepper to taste

Cook rice in the chicken stock until light and fluffy. (May be cooked ahead of time and set aside.) Sauté the nuts in the butter and salt until golden, about 5 minutes. Combine rice and nut mixture. Add salt and pepper. Sprinkle with nutmeg and serve.

Sautéed Sugar Snaps

▪••●••▪

2-1/2 pounds fresh sugar snap peas
2 tablespoons unsalted butter
1 teaspoon sugar
Salt to taste

Clean and stem peas. Sauté peas in butter until crisp-tender and still bright green. Sprinkle with sugar and salt. Serve immediately.

Strawberry Sweetheart Meringue Cake

Strawberry Sauce
3 pints fresh strawberries (reserve 1 pint for garnish)
1/4 cup sugar
1 tablespoon Crème de Cassis

White Cake
1/2 cup sugar
1 stick butter, softened
4 egg yolks
5 tablespoons milk
1 cup cake flour
1 teaspoon baking powder
Pinch of salt
1/2 teaspoon fresh lemon juice

Pecan Meringue Topping
4 egg whites
1 cup sugar
1/2 cup chopped pecans

Strawberry Filling
8 ounces fresh strawberries
1-1/2 cups whipping cream
3/4 teaspoon Crème de Cassis

Strawberry Sauce: Pureé 2 pints of strawberries, sugar and Crème de Cassis in blender and chill for several hours.

Cream butter and sugar until fluffy. Add egg yolks and beat until well blended. Sift flour, baking powder and salt. Alternate flour and milk to creamed mixture. Start and end with flour mixture. Add lemon juice. Spread in 2 9-inch, well-greased cake pans.

Prepare meringue by beating egg whites until foamy. Gradually add sugar and beat until very stiff. Spread meringue over cake batter and sprinkle with nuts. Bake at 300° for 30 to 35 minutes, or until lightly browned. Cool 10 minutes. Remove one layer and place upside down on plate (meringue on bottom). Whip cream with Crème de Cassis and spread layer with one half of cream. Slice strawberries and layer over cream. Place second cake layer on top with meringue facing up.

To serve: Spoon sauce on a plate and place a slice of cake on top. Garnish with a dollop of remaining whipped cream and decorate with a fresh strawberry.

MARDI GRAS SEAFOOD EXTRAVAGANZA

Oysters Washington

*Sautéed Crawfish on Mixed Greens
with Creole Andouille Sauce*

Queenie's Imperial Crab Gumbo

Pompano on Parade

Broiled Tomato Halves with Herbs and Gruyère

Braised Celery with Toasted Almonds

Apple Bread Pudding Soufflé with Whiskey Sauce

King Cake

Le café

SERVES 12

King Cake is traditionally served on the Feast of the Epiphany,

the "twelfth day of Christmas." This feast celebrates the coming of the three Kings,

setting off a round of celebrations for the Mardi Gras season.

No one can think of New Orleans without thinking of their culinary excellence,

the king and queen on a beautiful float, parades, costumes, jazz,

elegant homes, street cars and "let the good times roll."

Our "Seafood Extravaganza" highlights a potpourri

of specialties from the Bayou state.

With Mardi Gras colors being yellow, green and purple, you might

choose bouquets of daffodils and purple irises.

Continue the theme with yellow placemats and purple napkins.

Tie napkins with a plastic bead necklace which each guest

can wear during dinner. Sprinkle confetti, beads and doubloons on your table.

Use small gold crowns to hold placecards or, using gold paper,

cut out crowns and write guest names on each one.

Oysters Washington

—•○●○•—

1/4 cup fresh parsley
4 scallions
1 cup fresh spinach, packed
4 or 5 celery stalk tops with leaves
1/3 cup melted butter
1/3 cup bread crumbs
1 tablespoon Worcestershire sauce
1 tablespoon anchovy paste
Salt (if using washed oysters)
Cayenne pepper or a Louisiana hot sauce
2 tablespoons Pernod
Parmesan cheese, freshly grated

1 box rock salt (or ice cream salt)
2-1/2 to 3 dozen raw oysters, shucked *

Chop all greens in food processor. Add all remaining ingredients except cheese and process quickly. (This mixture may be prepared ahead of time and refrigerated). Taste for seasoning. Using large baking pans, line with the rock salt and place oyster shells on top of salt. Place one oyster in each shell, top with a spoonful of Washington sauce and sprinkle with cheese. Bake at 450° for 30 minutes, and broil for the last 2 minutes. Serve immediately.

When oysters in the shell are not available, other oven proof dishes or scallop shells may be used.

* The microwave method for shucking oysters: Place the oysters in a glass casserole dish. Put them in the microwave for 5 minutes on warm (30%). Remove and pry open and shuck at once. The oysters will still be raw.

Holding the oyster with a potholder mitt to protect your hand, insert the point of an oyster knife into the pointed, hinged end. When oyster has been opened, cut muscle to release and pry shell open. Cut oyster free and discard flat shell. Serve in other half.

❧

Pernod is an anise flavored liqueur from France. You may substitute sherry. However, we really like the Pernod with this recipe.

❧

"Why, then the world's mine oyster, which I with sword will open."

W. Shakespeare

Celebration Seasoning:

1 box free flowing salt
5 tablespoons ground black pepper
5 tablespoons ground cayenne (red) pepper
4 tablespoons pure garlic powder
3 tablespoons chili powder
2 tablespoons paprika

Mix well, use in a shaker and store the remainder in an airtight container. Use it like salt on meats, fish, soups, gumbos and salads. You may adjust the peppers to your taste.

Andouille is pork sausage highly seasoned with herbs, peppers and spices and is often used in Creole cooking.

Sautéed Crawfish on Mixed Greens with Creole Andouille Sauce

12 cups mixed greens
24 cherry tomatoes, cut in half
1 pound crawfish tails (usually available frozen in specialty shops, or substitute small peeled shrimp)
Tabasco or Louisiana hot sauce
1 cup flour
Celebration Seasoning *
1 tablespoon olive oil
1 tablespoon butter

Sauce
1/2 pound andouille sausage, casing removed
1/2 cup chopped onion
1 large clove minced garlic
1/2 cup red wine vinegar
2 teaspoons brown sugar
2 cups mayonnaise
1 tablespoon Creole mustard

In heavy skillet, crumble sausage while browning. Add chopped onion. Cook for 1 minute, add brown sugar, minced garlic, vinegar and a few dashes of hot sauce. Cook 1 minute longer. Cool slightly. Combine the mayonnaise and Creole mustard. Add sausage mixture and mix well. Season to taste with Celebration Seasoning. (This can be made up to 5 days ahead.) Toss crawfish tails in the hot sauce and allow to marinate while preparing greens and tomatoes. Mix Celebration Seasoning with flour and shake the crawfish tails in a bag to coat. Heat olive oil and butter in a large skillet, and sauté quickly until brown and crusty on the outside. Keep warm.

To serve: Arrange greens and cherry tomato halves on 12 plates. Spoon andouille sauce over salad and top with the hot crawfish. Serve immediately.

* See recipe for Celebration Seasoning, page 14 side note.

Queenie's Imperial Crab Gumbo

—•●●•—

Stock
2 to 3 pounds fresh fish bones (from seafood market)
    and/or 1/2 dozen fresh crabs
1 onion, quartered
1 stalk celery, halved
1 carrot
3 quarts water

Roux
1/2 cup flour
1/2 cup vegetable oil

Gumbo
1 cup chopped onions
1/2 cup chopped celery
1/2 cup chopped bell pepper
1 to 2 cloves minced garlic
2 tablespoons olive oil
1 pound fresh or frozen cut okra
1 cup chopped fresh tomatoes (or one small can)
1-1/2 pounds crabmeat, claw and lump (canned may
    be used in combination with fresh)
1/2 pound diced ham or smoked sausage
1/2 teaspoon thyme
1/2 teaspoon basil
1 bay leaf
1 tablespoon Celebration Seasoning (or to taste) *
1/4 cup chopped fresh parsley
3 to 4 cups cooked white rice (1-1/2 to 2 cups uncooked)

This is an okra gumbo, with okra being the thickening agent. A "Filé Gumbo" has no okra and the filé (ground sassafras leaves) is sprinkled over the gumbo when served. It does not make the gumbo hot and spicy, but flavors and thickens it.

In a large gumbo or soup pot, make stock by boiling all ingredients in 3 quarts of water. Shrimp and/or crab shells may be added for extra flavor. Simmer for about 2 hours and strain, reserving only the stock. This may be done ahead and refrigerated or frozen.)

To make roux: Mix flour and oil. Microwave on high for 6 minutes in microwave-safe quart size measuring cup. Stir well and cook an additional 30 seconds to brown the roux to a rich brown color. Additional time may be necessary to achieve this color.

Add onion, celery and bell pepper and cook 2 minutes. Add garlic and cook an additional 1 minute. Slowly whisk in 3 to 4 tablespoons hot water until smooth and blended. Using heavy covered pot (not a black iron one!) cook okra in olive oil over low heat for about 45 minutes until soft and no longer "ropey," stirring frequently. Add tomatoes and cook an additional 5 to 10 minutes. (Or cook in microwave on high for 25 minutes, stirring occasionally. Add tomatoes and cook an additional 5 minutes.) This may be done ahead of time and frozen or refrigerated until ready to use.

To assemble gumbo: Combine roux mixture with okra and gradually add stock while stirring. Add ham or sausage, herbs, salt, black and red pepper to taste. Stir in the crab meat and cook an additional 1/2 hour. Adjust seasonings. Add chopped parsley.

Spoon 1/4 cup rice in bowl and ladle gumbo over rice.

You may want to serve fresh French bread with this dinner.

* See recipe for Celebration Seasoning, page 14 side note.

Broiled Tomato Halves with Herbs and Gruyère

━━•◦●◦•━━

6 firm, ripe medium-sized tomatoes, halved with stemmed end removed
2 to 3 tablespoons extra virgin olive oil
3 tablespoons chopped fresh basil leaves (or 3 teaspoons dried)
1/2 to 3/4 cup grated Gruyère cheese
Salt and pepper to taste

Sprinkle tomato halves with salt, pepper and the chopped basil. Drizzle with the olive oil, and top with grated cheese. Broil for 10 minutes on second rack of oven so that tomato will heat through and cheese will be bubbly and begin to brown. Serve hot.

Braised Celery with Toasted Almonds

━━•◦●◦•━━

1 cup slivered almonds
4 tablespoons butter
1 teaspoon salt or celery salt
2 heads celery (with leaves), cut diagonally into 1/2 inch slices
3 teaspoons celery seeds
2/3 cup chicken broth
3 teaspoons lemon juice
White pepper to taste
2 teaspoons cornstarch, dissolved in 4 teaspoons water

In a small skillet, toast almonds in 2 tablespoons butter and celery salt, stirring until golden. Remove from heat. In a separate large skillet, cook celery pieces with celery seeds in the remaining butter over moderate heat for 1 to 2 minutes. Stir in broth, lemon juice and white pepper. Simmer covered for about 5 minutes. Add the cornstarch mixture and stir. Bring the liquid to a boil, sprinkle with the toasted almonds and serve.

Pompano on Parade

— • ○ ● ○ ■—

12 6-ounce skinned pompano fillets (sole or
    flounder may be substituted)
2 teaspoons salt (or to taste)
2 cups dry white wine
3 bay leaves
2 onions, sliced
Juice from 2 lemons
Parchment paper for papillotes

Sauce
1/3 cup butter
2 cups chopped scallions
2 pounds raw peeled and deveined shrimp
3 cups poaching liquid
1/3 cup flour
1/2 cup heavy cream
1/2 teaspoon ground cayenne pepper (or to taste)
1/2 teaspoon ground white pepper (or to taste)
1/3 cup butter

   Place fillets in a shallow pan with sliced onion, 2 cups white wine, bay leaves and lemon juice and water to just cover. Season with salt. Place in 350° oven for 7 to 8 minutes, or until fillets feel firm when touched with a finger. Transfer fish to a platter, and reserve the poaching liquid.

   Melt butter in skillet and sauté scallions until limp. Add the raw shrimp and 1 cup of the poaching liquid. Make a paste of the flour mixed with small amount of poaching liquid and gradually whisk into scallion and shrimp mixture. Stir in the remaining poaching liquid and heavy cream and cook until thickened seasoning with salt, white pepper and cayenne. Set aside.

   To make papillotes, fold a 10 inch length of parchment paper in half and cut heart shaped pieces 10 inches high and 14 inches wide. Unfold the parchment and brush surface with softened butter. Place one fillet on one side at the crease. Repeat for all 12 portions, and top each fillet with equal amounts of the sauce, being careful to distribute the shrimp evenly. Top with fresh parsley. Seal the edges by starting at the top of the heart and crimping together at 1/2 inch intervals. At the bottom point of the papillote, insert a drinking straw and blow in to inflate the paper, crimping immediately after removing straw.

   Place papillotes on a greased baking pan and bake in 400° oven for 15 minutes. The paper should begin to brown. Remove from oven. Cut an "X" in parchment and fold back edges to serve.

Parchment paper is a white, heat resistant paper sold in cookware stores.

A Mardi Gras parade always precedes the "Ball" of that Krewe such as Bacchus, Rex or Orpheus.

Apple Bread Pudding Soufflé with Whiskey Sauce

———•◦●◦•———

3 cups milk
1/2 stick butter
3/4 cup sugar
6 cups day old French bread, cubed
1/2 cup raisins
1-1/2 cups peeled and cubed apple
4 egg yolks, beaten
1/4 teaspoon salt
3/4 teaspoon grated nutmeg
1-1/2 teaspoons vanilla
6 egg whites
1/8 teaspoon cream of tartar
2 tablespoons sugar

Whiskey Sauce
1/2 stick butter
2 cups confectioners sugar
1/3 cup whiskey

Butter 2-quart soufflé dish or a 9 x 13 Pyrex dish. Preheat oven to 350°. Scald milk in microwave or on top of stove. Melt butter in milk and stir in sugar. Place cubed bread in a large bowl, add raisins and apples, and pour hot milk mixture over bread. Stir well and let stand for 15 minutes. Add salt, nutmeg and vanilla to egg yolks and mix well into bread. Beat egg whites with cream of tartar (unless you have a copper bowl, in which case you will not need the cream of tartar) and after soft peaks form, gradually add the sugar, beating until dissolved. Stir about one fourth of the meringue into the bread mixture, then gently fold in the remaining meringue. Carefully pour into the prepared baking dish and bake for 45 minutes.

For whiskey sauce: Melt butter, add sugar and whiskey. Stir to blend.

To serve: Spoon soufflé into stemmed glass and top with whiskey sauce.

King Cake

1/2 cup water
1/2 cup milk
1/2 cup sugar
2 teaspoons salt
5 eggs
1/2 cup butter
4-1/2 cups bread flour
1/4 to 1/2 teaspoon grated nutmeg
1/2 teaspoon mace
2-1/2 teaspoons (one envelope) active dry yeast

Glaze
4 ounces softened cream cheese
2 cups confectioners sugar
2 to 4 tablespoons milk, or as much as needed for spreading consistency
Green, yellow and purple granulated sugar (Each color mixed separately in a plastic sandwich bag with a few drops of food coloring or colored sugars can also be purchased.)

Bread machine method: Put ingredients in large bread machine pan in the order given and set to DOUGH and FIRST RISE cycle. This is usually about 1 hour 40 minutes. Remove from pan and put on floured board, punching down and working in more flour as needed. Make one long strip with the dough (about 18 to 24 inches long) and cut into 3 equal strips, leaving one end attached. Braid the dough and place on a greased large cookie sheet in a wide circle, placing a round oven-proof pan about 4 to 5 inches in diameter in the center (to maintain a ring). Hide a small plastic baby or a large bean somewhere in the cake. Brush with oil, cover with a clean towel and let rise for an hour or more or until double in size. Bake at 375° for 25 to 30 minutes.

Food processor method: Proof the yeast in the milk and water (115°) with a pinch of sugar until yeast is completely dissolved. Place half the flour, sugar, salt, nutmeg and mace (optional) in food processor with steel blade and process until mixture resembles cornmeal. Add the warm yeast mixture and blend by turning the machine on and off very quickly. Add one egg, start processor, and continue to add the rest of the eggs with the motor running. Add additional flour while the motor is running but dough should be somewhat sticky. Pour dough out onto floured board or surface, rub a little oil on top and cover with a piece of plastic wrap, then a clean kitchen towel. Let rise until double in size. Proceed as stated above to form and bake the King Cake.

For glaze: Stir cream cheese until very soft, gradually add sugar. Add milk as needed until desired consistency. Glaze the warm cake, while still warm, alternate the three colored sugars in whatever pattern you choose.

To serve: Allow each person to choose his piece of cake. The one that has the baby or bean in his piece is the "king," and will have the next "King Cake" party.

Le Café

Freshly brewed dark roast coffee, served in demitasse cups.

RAINY NIGHT IN LONDON

Mushroom Terrine

Artichokes Alistair

Oyster and Spinach Cream Soup

*Watercress and Grape Salad with
Toasted Nuts and Lemon Cream Dressing*

Sautéed Veal Chops with Stilton and Currant Sauce

Fanned New Potatoes and Fresh Tarragon

English Peas in Radicchio Cups

Derbyshire Bakewell Tart

SERVES 12

Oh, to be in England, with moated castles and well-tended gardens....
British cooking and weather have always been the subject of many jokes,
however, recent holidays to England have proven their cuisine can be "jolly good."
This menu should prove just how good it can be!

A wonderful centerpiece for this "Rainy Night In London"
menu would be a combination of fruits and vegetables piled high in your
favorite porcelain bowl or basket. A large red cabbage with its leaves
spread slightly open surrounded by artichokes, mushrooms, pomegranates and
pears set the color theme. Drape red and green grapes over the side of the container.
Blossoms and ivy, placed in florist vials, can be tucked between the vegetables
to create your own Flemish painting. Continue the theme by placing more grapes
and vegetables around the bowl.
Hollowed out fresh artichokes make charming votive candle holders.
Place one at every or every other place. To complete the setting,
combine the rich warm colors of your centerpiece for your placemats and napkins.
This lovely tablescape should chase away the winter blues.

Mushroom Terrine

—•◦●◦•—

8 ounces mushrooms, cleaned and sliced
2 ounces butter
2 tablespoons bread crumbs
2 teaspoons finely grated onion
3 ounces softened butter
4 ounces light cream cheese
1/8 teaspoon nutmeg
1 teaspoon lemon juice
Salt and freshly ground black pepper
Fresh sprigs of watercress

Melt 2 ounces butter in skillet and add mushrooms. Stir and cook until softened and reduced, about 15 minutes. Stir in bread crumbs and allow to cool. Add mixture to blender or food processor along with the onion, softened butter, cheese, nutmeg, lemon juice. Salt and pepper to taste. Blend and remove it to a terrine or mold lined with plastic wrap or foil. Cover with plastic wrap and chill until set. To unmold, wrap a hot, damp cloth around the dish to loosen the terrine. Repeat if necessary and invert on serving dish and garnish with watercress.

Serve with crackers or thinly sliced baguettes.

This is a wonderful alternative to a meat paté. It is an excellent first course or a perfect picnic spread for French bread.

To store mushrooms, choose a container that will let them breathe. Never wash mushrooms before storing as they will absorb water and deteriorate quickly. Clean them before serving by wiping with a damp cloth, paper towel or mushroom brush.

Artichokes Alistair

24 artichoke bottoms (approximately 3 cans)

Sauce
3 tablespoons olive oil
2 onions, chopped
4 tomatoes peeled, seeded and chopped
2 bay leaves
4 sprigs of fresh thyme
2/3 cup dry white wine

Stuffing
6 ounces proscuitto, chopped
2/3 cup semi-dry bread, crust removed, soaked in water
　　and squeezed dry and chopped
4 tablespoons parsley, chopped
2 cloves garlic, minced
3/4 cup Parmesan cheese, grated
1 egg, beaten
3 tablespoons butter, melted
Salt and pepper to taste

　　Heat oil in heavy skillet. Add onions and cook 10 minutes. Add tomatoes, bay leaves, thyme and wine. Pour into a 9 x 13 inch pan.

　　For stuffing, combine all ingredients and fill each artichoke bottom with a rounded spoon of stuffing. Place evenly on top of tomato mixture. Sprinkle with salt and pepper and drizzle melted butter on top.

　　Bake covered for 15 minutes at 350°. Uncover and bake for 25 minutes or until sauce is reduced. Broil 1 minute to brown tops slightly. Serve 2 bottoms on each plate with sauce underneath. Garnish with sprigs of fresh thyme.

Oyster and Spinach Cream Soup

— ∎•●•∎ —

1 quart raw oysters
2 to 3 bunches fresh spinach (or 2 pounds frozen chopped)
6 tablespoons butter
2/3 cup chopped onion
1 clove minced garlic
2 stalks chopped celery
6 tablespoons flour
1/2 teaspoon garlic salt
3/4 teaspoon Celebration Seasoning *
Pinch of nutmeg
2 tablespoons white wine Worcestershire sauce
2 tablespoons sherry
1/2 teaspoon or more to taste cayenne pepper
Salt and white pepper to taste
1 quart milk
1 quart light cream
Fresh spinach for garnish

Cook oysters in 3 cups of water until done, approximately 5 minutes or until curled. Drain oysters, save liquid and keep it hot. Chop oysters in quarters and set aside. Melt butter and sauté onions, celery and garlic, stirring constantly until cooked. Push aside and sprinkle flour over butter and stir to make a paste. Pour in hot oyster liquid, stirring until smooth. Add fresh spinach and cook for 30 minutes. Add garlic salt, nutmeg, Worcestershire sauce, sherry, cayenne, Celebration Seasoning, salt and pepper. Add milk and cream and cook over low heat until very hot but not boiling. Add oysters and continue cooking 5 to 7 minutes. Serve and garnish with slivers of fresh spinach.

* See recipe for Celebration Seasoning, page 14, side note.

This soup is usually pureed but we like it chunky, and don't skimp on the seasoning!

Fanned New Potatoes with Fresh Tarragon

12 medium new potatoes (or 24 small)
1/2 cup melted butter
2 tablespoons fresh chopped tarragon
1/4 cup fresh Parmesan cheese

Slice potatoes in thin slices but do not cut all the way through. Fan potatoes and place in 9 x 13 casserole dish. Spoon 1/4 cup of the melted butter over potatoes. Bake for 45 minutes at 375°. Baste potatoes with remaining butter and sprinkle with tarragon and cheese. Bake for 10 more minutes or until done and lightly brown.

English Peas in Radicchio Cups

1 cup chicken stock
4 green onions, sliced, including some of the tops
1/2 teaspoon sugar
3 pounds fresh English peas, shelled
3 tablespoons butter
Salt and freshly ground pepper
12 small radicchio leaves

In a saucepan, bring stock, onions and sugar to a simmer. Add the peas and simmer for 5 minutes until tender. Drain, add butter and cook 1 minute. Have radicchio leaves at room temperature. Place a radicchio leaf on each plate and fill with a portion of hot peas. Serve immediately.

Derbyshire Bakewell Tart

Crust
3/4 cup all purpose flour
6 tablespoons cake flour
1/4 cup sugar
Pinch of salt
1/2 cup salted butter
3 to 4 tablespoons cold water

Filling
1/2 cup unsalted butter
1/2 cup sugar
1-1/2 cups ground almonds
2 tablespoons flour
3 large eggs, beaten
2 tablespoons Amaretto liqueur
1/2 cup seedless raspberry jam

Topping
1 cup whipping cream
1 tablespoon Amaretto

Sliced almonds and fresh raspberries for garnish

Preheat oven to 350°. Blend first four ingredients in food processor. Add butter cut in pieces using off/on switch until mixture resembles fine meal. Blend in water by the tablespoon. Form dough into a ball and chill for 30 minutes. Roll out on sheets of waxed paper to 1/8-inch thickness. Transfer to a 9-inch tart pan with removable bottom. Trim edges and freeze for 15 minutes. Line shell with foil and fill with dried beans or pie weights. Bake at 350° for 20 minutes. Remove foil and bake until brown, about 10 minutes. Cool. (Can be made the day ahead).

Beat butter and sugar until blended. Mix ground almonds and flour in together. Add eggs and almond mixture alternately to butter mixture, beating well. Stir in liqueur. Spread jam over crust. Spread egg and butter mixture over jam. Decorate with sliced almonds. Bake until filling is set and top is golden, about 35 minutes. Cool to room temperature. Whip cream with Amaretto. Cut tart in 2 inch portions and top with a dollop of cream and fresh raspberries.

The term "pudding" in England refers to most desserts, pies, tarts, creams and trifles as well as baked and steamed puddings.

This Bakewell Tart is named after a town in Derbyshire, England. The story goes that it was invented in the 19th century, quite by accident. It is an easy-to-make jam, custard and almond delight. We added the liqueur and cream for our own version of this English "pudding."

A FIRESIDE AFFAIR

Warmed Herb Cheese Spread

Sherried Mushroom Strudel

Corn and Crab Bisque

Mixed Winter Greens with Chutney Dijon Dressing

Roast Duckling with Blackberry Sauce

Carrot Soufflé

Braised Brussels Sprouts with Chestnuts and Shallots

Walnut Crème Gâteau

SERVES 12

Quickly — Come Inside!

Join us on this cold, blustery evening.

The rich aroma of roasted duckling greets us,

laughter is heard in the distance and

the warmth of a roaring fire beckons us

to shed our coats and join in the merriment.

Personal collections reflect the personality of the host and are often

included in our table settings. Take this opportunity to display crystal candlesticks

of all shapes and sizes. A vintage lace tablecloth would make the perfect backdrop,

tuck tiny crystal objects between the candlesticks and add gold candles.

A low crystal bowl filled with white tulips

compliments the masses of flickering candles

and creates a magical setting.

Warmed Herb Cheese Spread

— •• ● •• —

1 package (3 ounces) cream cheese, softened
1 cup grated sharp yellow Cheddar cheese
1 cup grated Muenster cheese
2 tablespoons Dijon mustard
4 scallions, finely chopped
1/8 cup chives, finely chopped
1/8 cup parsley, finely chopped
1 garlic clove, crushed
4 or more unpeeled apples, cut in slices

    Preheat oven to 375°. Mix all ingredients except apples thoroughly. Place mixture in small ovenproof baking dish. Bake for 15 to 20 minutes. Serve with apple slices.

    May also be served cold. Divide mixture in half. Roll each half in a mix of finely chopped parsley and finely chopped chives.

Sherried Mushroom Strudel

1 pound fresh mushrooms, thinly sliced
1 small onion, chopped
2 tablespoons butter or margarine
3/4 teaspoon salt
1/8 teaspoon pepper
1 tablespoon cream sherry
4 ounces cream cheese
1 teaspoon fresh dill or 1/2 teaspoon dill weed
1 tablespoon dry bread crumbs
6 frozen phyllo sheets, thawed
Melted butter
1 tablespoon dry bread crumbs
Fresh marjoram sprigs

Sauté mushrooms and onion in 2 tablespoons butter in large skillet until mushrooms are tender, about 3 minutes. Stir in salt, pepper, sherry, cream cheese and dill. Stir until smooth. Remove from heat. Stir in bread crumbs. Cool to room temperature.

Heat oven to 375°. Layer 3 phyllo sheets on damp kitchen towel, brushing each layer with melted butter. Spoon half the mushroom mixture on short end of phyllo sheet turning in long sides of sheet about one inch to keep filling in place. Lift towel, using it to roll sheet like a jelly roll starting from narrow end closest to filling. Place roll, seam side down, on lightly buttered jelly roll pan. Brush top and sides of dough with melted butter. Sprinkle with bread crumbs. Repeat procedure with remaining ingredients. Bake strudel until brown and crisp, 30 to 35 minutes. Let cool slightly. Cut each strudel into six pieces. Garnish with fresh marjoram.

If you have a bit of a heavy hand with the salt shaker when making a sauce or salad dressing, it can be corrected. Just add some type of acid such as wine vinegar, lemon or lime juice.

Corn and Crab Bisque

—•◦•◦•—

3/4 cup butter
2 1/4 cups chopped green onion tops
3 tablespoons all purpose flour
2 teaspoons Celebration Seasoning *
2 cloves garlic, minced
1 teaspoon fresh thyme
1-1/2 quarts (6 cups) fish stock **
10 ears fresh corn, cut from the cob,
     or 3 12-ounce cans whole kernel corn, drained
2 cups whipping cream
1 pound lump crabmeat
Fresh thyme sprigs

   Melt butter in large saucepan over medium heat. Add onion and garlic and sauté until wilted. Stir in flour, Celebration Seasoning, garlic and thyme and continue cooking until flour begins to stick to pan. Blend in fish stock, reduce heat and simmer until stock thickens, about 15 minutes. Add corn and simmer an additional 15 minutes. Slowly stir in cream and blend well. Gently add crabmeat. Remove from heat and let stand 30 minutes. Reheat gently over low heat, being careful crabmeat does not break up into flakes and cream does not curdle.
   To serve: Garnish with a fresh sprig of thyme.
   * See recipe for Celebration Seasoning, page 14, side note.

** *Fish Stock*
2 quarts (8 cups) water
Fish bones or 1 lb. shrimp in shells ***
10 celery stalks
3 medium onions, quartered
2-1/4 tablespoons liquid crab boil (available in specialty food stores)

   Combine all ingredients in large saucepan and bring to boil. Reduce heat and simmer 3 hours, adding water as necessary to make 1-1/2 quarts stock. Strain and cool.
   *** Ask your fishmonger for fish bones.

Candle wicks should always be charred before guests arrive. Unlit wicks are considered to be a sign of inhospitality.

❧

"Some people come into our lives and quickly go; some stay for a while, leave footprints on our hearts, and we are never, ever the same."

Flavia Weed

Homemade croûtons can be done in a jiffy and they are so much better than packaged ones. Sauté one clove minced garlic in 2 tablespoons olive oil. Cut your leftover French or Italian bread into cubes. Add to pan and brown, stirring occasionally. Watch so they don't burn!

An old Spanish proverb says, "Four persons are wanted to make a good salad; a spendthrift for oil, a miser for vinegar, a counselor for salt and a madman to stir it all up!"

Mixed Winter Greens
with Chutney Dijon Dressing

Dressing
3/4 cup salad oil
1/4 cup white wine vinegar
1 teaspoon sugar
1 teaspoon salt
1 teaspoon Dijon mustard
2 tablespoons chutney
1/2 teaspoon freshly ground black pepper
1/2 teaspoon garlic powder
1 teaspoon Worcestershire sauce
2 tablespoons fresh lemon juice

8 to 10 cups fresh greens
3 tomatoes, chopped
2 cups croûtons

Place oil and vinegar in blender. Mix remaining ingredients in a small bowl and then add to oil and vinegar. Mix briefly. Chill well. Makes 2 cups.

Serve over a mixture of fresh greens (bibb, romaine, red and green leaf lettuce). Add chopped fresh tomatoes and homemade croûtons.

Roast Duckling with Blackberry Sauce

Duckling
3 dressed ducklings, 5 1/2 pounds each
3 small onions, quartered and peeled
3 small apples, quartered, skin on
1-1/2 teaspoon salt
1/2 teaspoon pepper

Sauce
1-1/2 quarts water
3 cups coarsely chopped onion
1-1/2 cups chopped celery
1-1/2 cups chopped carrots
3 16-ounce cans blackberries, undrained
1/3 cup Cointreau
1/3 cup blackberry jam
1-1/2 tablespoons all purpose flour
1-1/2 tablespoons butter, softened

Remove giblets and neck from ducklings, set aside. Prick the skin of fatty areas of ducklings with fork. Stuff each cavity with quartered onion and apples. Close cavity with skewers. Sprinkle with salt and pepper. Fold neck skin under and place ducklings, breast side up, on a rack in a large roasting pan. Bake, uncovered, at 350° for 2 hours or until drumsticks and thighs move easily. Discard onions and apples. Set aside and keep warm.

Combine reserved giblets and neck, water, chopped onion, celery and carrots in medium saucepan. Bring to a boil, stirring well. Reduce heat, cover and simmer 20 to 25 minutes. Drain and reserve 2/12 cups stock. Discard giblets, neck and vegetables. Drain blackberries, reserve 2-1/2 cups juice and set aside. Combine scrapings from roasting pan, reserved blackberry juice, Cointreau and reserved duck stock in medium saucepan. Bring to a boil and boil 15 minutes or until liquid is reduced by half. Make a paste by combining jam, flour and butter and gradually add to liquid in pan, stirring well. Cook over medium heat, stirring constantly, until thickened. Stir in blackberries.

Cut ducklings into quarters, place under broiler to crisp skin. Transfer to serving platter and serve with blackberry sauce.

Leftover sauce can be frozen.

"Good company, good wine, good welcome make good people...."

W. Shakespeare

"The hostess must be like the duck – calm and unruffled on the surface and paddling like hell underneath."

Anonymous

While the word soufflé means "puffed," it refers to a hot or cold dish with a light texture that uses beaten egg whites to achieve height.

"Chestnuts roasting on an open fire" certainly conjures up cozy winter memories. The lowly Brussels sprout becomes a gourmet delight in this presentation.

To speed cooking time of Brussels sprouts, cut a 1/4 inch cross into trimmed stems.

Carrot Soufflé

3 eggs, separated
1 tablespoon sugar
1-1/2 tablespoon cornstarch
1 cup milk
3 cups (2 pounds) carrots, cooked and mashed
3 tablespoons butter
1 teaspoon salt
1 cup fine bread crumbs
1 cup light cream
1/2 teaspoon grated nutmeg
1/4 cup cream sherry

Preheat oven to 300°. Grease a 2 quart casserole. Lightly beat egg yolks and sugar. Mix cornstarch with small amount of milk; heat remaining milk, add cornstarch and stir until smooth and slightly thickened. Stir small amount of hot cornstarch mixture into egg yolks and sugar. Stir to mix well; then return to hot milk, cooking and stirring over medium heat until smooth and thick. Add carrots, butter, salt and bread crumbs, blend evenly. Stir in cream, and add nutmeg and sherry and mix well. Beat egg whites until they hold firm peaks, fold into carrot mixture. Pour into casserole. Place in pan of hot water and bake at 300° for 30 minutes. Increase heat to 350° and bake and additional 45 minutes or until knife inserted in center comes out clean.

Braised Brussels Sprouts
with Chestnuts and Shallots

1/4 cup butter
4 to 6 shallots, peeled and finely chopped
1-1/2 cups chicken broth
2 bay leaves
2 pounds fresh brussels sprouts, trimmed or 2 pounds frozen
16 ounces whole roasted chestnuts in jars
Salt and pepper to taste

Melt butter in heavy sauce pan over medium high heat. Add shallots and cook until golden brown, stirring occasionally. Add broth and bay leaves.

Add chestnuts to shallots, cover and simmer until chestnuts are tender, about 4 minutes. Add Brussels sprouts to shallots. Boil until Brussels sprouts are tender and liquid is syrupy. Season with salt and pepper and serve.

Walnut Crème Gâteau

— •• • • ■ —

Gâteau
12 large eggs, separated
2 cups sugar
4 tablespoons fine bread crumbs
4 cups ground walnuts, reserving a few walnut halves for garnish
1 teaspoon salt
2 tablespoons vanilla

Crème
1-1/2 pints whipping cream
1 teaspoon vanilla
3 tablespoons brown sugar

    In large bowl, beat 12 egg yolks with 1 cup sugar until thick and fluffy (about 10 minutes, do not overbeat). Fold in vanilla, walnuts, bread crumbs and salt. Beat egg whites and remaining 1 cup sugar until satiny. Fold egg yolk mixture into egg whites. Sprinkle bottom of 4 cake pans, 8 inch size, with salt and lay a layer of waxed paper on top of salt. Divide the batter into the cake pans. Bake at 350° for 25 minutes and cool. Whip the cream, add vanilla and brown sugar. Run a knife around the edges of the cake pans and remove to serving plates. Spread crème between layers, on tops and sides and serve. Decorate with walnut halves.

"If Winter comes, can Spring be far behind..."

"Ode To The West Wind"
Percy Shelley

❧

A flourless cake gets its substance from the ground nuts and eggs.

❧

You may choose to have dessert and coffee at the table, however, moving to another room allows your guests to stretch their legs and lets the party start all over again.

NOTES:

Spring

GOURMET IN BLOOM

Roasted Elephant Garlic Flowerette

Mussel Velouté with Saffron and Fennel

Spring Asparagus Salad

*Sherried Tenderloin of Beef
with Currants and Green Peppercorn Sauce*

Tarragon Carrots by Crispin

Rosemary New Potatoes

Almond Frangelico Ice Cream Torte

SERVES 12

Over the years, a few of the gardeners in our group have been transformed

into cooks and likewise, some of our cooks have become passionate gardeners.

We now share both recipes and cuttings!

Many of our planning sessions begin with a walk through the hostess' garden.

Our centerpieces have evolved from the very formal

to creative arrangements composed of flowers,

greenery and herbs from our gardens.

Masses of pastel flowers form a color palette that is reminiscent

of Monet's garden. Using a powder pink tablecloth as a backdrop,

fill the table with every blooming variety from your garden

(or floral shop). A small vintage hatbox or basket

with a plastic liner can be used as a container, with a lace-edged napkin or

doily draped over the side. Add an artist's palette with a few brushes

placed among the blossoms...this is a whimsical setting sure to please!

Roasted Elephant Garlic Flowerette

• • • •

4 large elephant garlic heads
3 tablespoons extra virgin olive oil
Salt and freshly ground pepper
Sprigs of fresh thyme for garnish
Balsamic vinegar
Baguettes of French bread, sliced and toasted

Peel the outside skin off each garlic head. Slice a thin top off the garlic to reveal cloves without detaching them. Place garlic on a sheet of aluminum foil. Brush each head with oil and season with salt and pepper. Sprinkle with balsamic vinegar. Wrap with foil to form a package. Bake on a baking sheet in preheated 300° oven until flesh is soft, approximately one-and-one-half hours.

To serve: Place on serving plate garnished with fresh thyme. Squeeze the flesh from the cloves, spread on crusty French bread.

A possible accompaniment to the garlic would be to chop a large fresh tomato and mix it with 2 tablespoons of chopped fresh basil. Serve as a topper for the roasted garlic. Another possible suggestion would be to spread softened goat cheese on bread, top with garlic, then chopped tomatoes.

Chèvre (goat cheese) is a pungent delicacy made from the milk of the wily goat and usually aged only a month. Though native of many parts of the world, chevre is the pride of Provence. In France, chèvre, married with a good wine, is an exquisite finale to dinner.

"Won't you come into my garden? I would like my roses to see you."

Richard Sheridan

Attractive garlic bakers are available in most cooking stores. You can bake and serve in the same container.

Mussel Velouté with Saffron and Fennel

2 tablespoons olive oil
3 medium fennel bulbs, trimmed and thinly sliced
2 small onions, chopped
1 cup chopped celery
4 garlic cloves, chopped
8 cups bottled clam juice
1 teaspoon saffron threads
2 bay leaves
2 cups dry white wine
5 pounds mussels, scrubbed and debearded
2 cups whipping cream
1/2 cup chopped fresh chives

Sauté fennel, onion, celery and garlic in heated oil until tender, about 14 minutes. Add clam juice, saffron and bay leaves. Reduce heat and simmer 45 minutes. Remove bay leaves. Set aside.

Bring wine to boil in large pot. Add mussels. Cover and steam about 5 minutes, until mussels open. Discard any unopened mussels. Transfer mussels to bowl and strain liquid. Purée liquid and sautéed vegetables until smooth. (May be prepared one day ahead of time. Cover mussels and soup separately. Refrigerate.)

Combine soup and cream. Bring to a simmer. Remove shells, leaving a few in the shells for garnish. Add mussels to soup and stir until heated through. Season with salt and pepper, sprinkle with chives.

Spring Asparagus Salad

3 pounds fresh asparagus, blanched
1 cup olive oil
6 tablespoons freshly squeezed lemon juice
2 tablespoons anchovy paste
2 teaspoons seasoned salt
2 teaspoons grated onion
1 clove garlic, crushed
3 teaspoons fresh chervil or 1 teaspoon dried
Salad greens, your choice
Sliced cherry tomatoes or red pepper rings

Cook asparagus in large pot of boiling water until crisp-tender, about 2 minutes. Drain. Rinse with cold water to cool; drain well.

Arrange in layers in deep bowl. Combine oil, lemon juice, anchovy paste, seasoned salt, onion, garlic and chervil in blender. Blend until mixed and pour over asparagus. Cover and refrigerate 4 to 6 hours. Remove the asparagus and arrange on crisp salad greens.

Garnish with sliced cherry tomatoes or red pepper rings.

Lemon Aid – Room temperature lemons will yield more juice than cold ones. If they are cold, prick the skin with a fork and place in the microwave for 30 seconds on high before juicing. It also helps to roll them around on the counter. This will give you even more juice.

"In his garden every man may be his own artist without apology or explanation. Here is the one spot where each may experience 'the romance of possibility'."

Louise Beebe Wilder

The flavor of the chervil herb is warm, part anise and part parsley.

Sherried Tenderloin of Beef with Currants and Green Peppercorn Sauce

6 cups beef stock
Salt and pepper to taste
3/4 to 1 tablespoon browning enhancer
3 tablespoons butter, softened
2 tablespoons walnut or olive oil
2 tenderloins of beef, trimmed, about 5 pounds each
2 carrots, sliced
1 medium to large onion, sliced
4 sprigs celery leaves
2 cups dry sherry
1/2 cup dried currants
2 tablespoons cracked green peppercorns
1 cup light cream
Fresh rosemary sprigs

Boil stock in heavy saucepan until reduced to 2 cups, about 10 minutes. Set aside. Season beef with salt and pepper. Mix browning enhancer with oil and butter. Rub mixture on tenderloins. Add carrots, onion and celery leaves to roasting pan. Place tenderloins on top of vegetables and roast in 425° oven for 15 minutes. Reduce temperature to 350° and cook for another 15 to 20 minutes for rare. Use instant reading meat thermometer. Insert on a slant into thickest part of meat to test for doneness, thermometer should read 125° to 130° for rare and 135° for medium rare. Transfer beef to platter and tent with foil to keep warm. Remove vegetables.

In pan with drippings, add sherry, currants and peppercorns. Boil until liquid is reduced by half, stirring occasionally, about 5 minutes. Add stock and cream and boil until thickened. Slice beef and spoon sauce over top. Garnish with fresh rosemary sprigs.

Tarragon Carrots by Crispin

4 tablespoons butter
2 medium onions, sliced
12 carrots, peeled and julienned
2 tablespoons sugar
1/2 cup fresh tarragon or 3 tablespoons dried and crumbled
Salt and pepper to taste

Melt butter in heavy skillet over medium heat. Add onions and sauté until soft, approximately 3 minutes. Increase heat to medium high, add carrots and sauté until just crisp, about 5 minutes. Stir in sugar and tarragon, cook an additional 2 minutes. Season with salt and pepper.

Rosemary New Potatoes

1 cup cider or malt vinegar
8 cups water
1 teaspoon salt
1/4 cup olive oil
3 pounds washed new potatoes, sliced
2 tablespoons fresh rosemary or 2-1/2 teaspoon dried
Garlic powder

Heat oven to 450°. Combine vinegar, water and salt in bowl with potatoes. Soak for 20 to 30 minutes; drain and dry. Toss potatoes with oil to coat. Arrange in single layer on two lightly oiled baking sheets. Bake at 450° 10 to 15 minutes or until brown underneath. Sprinkle with rosemary and garlic powder. Turn over and bake on other side until brown. Sprinkle with additional salt and pepper to taste.

The joy of growing fresh herbs will add to your cooking pleasure while enhancing the flavor of your food. Herbs are fun to grow and you don't need a lot of space. They can be grown in clay pots, window boxes or added to your garden plan. Plant the ones you use the most – dill, thyme, oregano, parsley, chives, basil and sage. At the end of your growing season, purée herbs with a little oil and freeze in plastic bags, each labeled for later use.

❦

Use two or three times the quantity of fresh herbs when substituting for dried, since the flavor is much more subtle.

Almond Frangelico Ice Cream Torte

─────────── ◦◦●●◦◦ ───────────

Frangelico is made from wild hazelnuts growing in the woods, exquisitely blended with the infusions of other berries and flowers to enrich the flavor.

Crust
8 tablespoons butter
1/4 cup sugar
1/4 cup semi-sweet chocolate chips
1 egg, beaten
1 cup flour

Filling
3/4 cup sliced almonds, lightly chopped
5 tablespoons Frangelico liqueur
2 ounces imported white chocolate
2 quarts premium vanilla ice cream

Topping
1 cup lightly sweetened whipping cream
1-1/2 cups semi-sweet chocolate chips
1 tablespoon butter
2 to 4 tablespoons water
12 fresh strawberries (slice whole berry and slightly fan)

For crust: Melt butter, sugar and chocolate chips over low heat. Let cool slightly and blend in egg and flour. Press mixture into bottom of a lightly greased 10 inch spring form pan. Bake at 375° for 6 to 7 minutes until slightly firm to touch. Center will be soft.   Cool.

For filling: Brush almonds with 2 tablespoons Frangelico. Lightly toast in oven at 250° and cool. Break white chocolate into small pieces and chop in food processor until very fine. Soften ice cream to a workable consistency. Blend chocolate, almonds, ice cream and 3 tablespoons Frangelico thoroughly. Pour mixture into cooled crust and freeze at least 6 hours.

When ready to serve, whip the cream. Melt the chocolate chips, butter and water over low heat to a pourable consistency. Cool. Drizzle sauce over individual servings. Garnish with a dollop of whipped cream and fluted strawberry.

APRIL IN PARIS

Petite Pinwheels

Coquille St. Jacques avec Champignon

Brie Bisque

Evantail Française

Sea Bass En Croûte with Shallot Hollandaise

Haricots Verts

Crêpes De Fraises Royale

SERVES 12

Cole Porter said it best, "I love Paris in the springtime...
I love Paris every moment of the year."

Transport your guests to Paris for this spring dinner by
setting your tables in the style of a French bistro.
Les Deux Magots, where Jake Barnes meets Lady Brett
in Hemingway's "The Sun Also Rises" might be your first stop.

Continue the theme by using two round tables covered with floor length
natural cotton or burlap cloths. Rusticity need not preclude elegance.
A table set with French faience and damask napkins tied
with ivy sprigs will continue the mood. A country French basket
filled with pink hyacinths, forced to bloom, look charming
surrounded by sphagnum moss and variegated ivy.
For an authentic touch, suggest that your guests wear berets and play the
"Best of Edith Piaf" in the background.

Petite Pinwheels

8 ounces cream cheese, softened
1/3 cup grated Parmesan cheese
2 green onions, sliced (green and white parts)
1 cup basil pesto (homemade or purchased) *
1 package frozen puff pastry, thawed until flexible
1/2 cup chopped ripe olives, drained well

Combine cream cheese, Parmesan cheese, green onions, and pesto; mix well. On a lightly floured surface, roll out each puff pastry sheet into a 10 x 16 inch rectangle. (There should be two sheets of pastry in each package.) Spread cream cheese mixture evenly over pastry sheets, completely covering them. Sprinkle half the olives on each sheet. Roll up each sheet like a jelly roll.

Freeze rolls at least 3 hours, or up to 2 months. When ready to bake, remove roll(s) from freezer and let thaw 15 to 30 minutes, then slice into 1/3 inch rounds. Put rounds on lightly greased baking sheet. Bake in a preheated 400° oven 12 to 15 minutes, or until lightly browned. Serve warm. May want to turn pinwheels to brown evenly. One roll will be sufficient to serve 12 people. Freeze the other roll for a treat at a later time.

* *Pesto*

1/4 cup pignolia nuts (pine nuts)
2 cloves garlic, peeled
1 teaspoon salt
1/2 teaspoon freshly ground pepper
2 cups fresh basil leaves, lightly packed
1/3 cup freshly grated Parmesan cheese
1/4 cup freshly grated Pecorino or Romano cheese
3/4 to 1 cup fine olive oil

In a food processor, grind all ingredients until fine with 1/2 cup of the olive oil. Add remaining oil and process until smooth and creamy. Use pesto immediately or refrigerate for up to 4 days. May be frozen.

"If I had but two loaves of bread, I would sell one and buy hyacinths, for they would feed my soul."

    The Koran

Ernest Hemingway referred to Paris as a "movable feast."

Extra pesto may be used with pasta or on pizza.

Coquille St. Jacques avec Champignon

2 tablespoons butter
1 tablespoon olive oil
2 cups sliced mushrooms
3 tablespoons shallots, minced
2 garlic cloves, minced
8 ounces mild Roquefort
1/2 cup white wine
1-1/2 pounds bay scallops
Parsley to garnish

Heat butter and olive oil; sauté mushrooms and shallots in heavy pan, adding minced garlic. Continue to sauté for 1 to 2 minutes. Blend mixture with cheese and wine until heated. Place the scallops equally into 12 ramekins or scallop shells. Top with the cheese mixture. Bake at 350° until bubbly, approximately 15 to 20 minutes.

To serve: Garnish with parsley.

Brie Bisque

2 pounds Brie cheese
3 cans (14 ounces each) chicken broth
3 tablespoons butter or margarine
12 ounces shiitake or cremini mushrooms
4 medium carrots, peeled and julienned
3 medium shallots, minced
3 cups light cream
3 tablespoons dry sherry
1/2 to 1 teaspoon cracked white pepper
Watercress sprigs for garnish
1 baguette loaf French bread cut in 1/2 inch cubes
1/2 cup olive oil
4 cloves garlic, sliced

Trim off and discard rind from Brie. In a large pan, bring broth to a boil. Add Brie and stir until smooth. Strain mixture and discard solids. Sauté mushrooms, carrots and shallots until tender, about 5 minutes. Stir in Brie mixture, cream, pepper, and sherry. Cover and simmer for 10 minutes.

Sauté garlic briefly. Remove the garlic and discard, add the bread cubes and sauté until lightly browned.

To serve: Ladle the bisque into bowls, garnish with watercress and sprinkle with croûtons.

Evantail Française
(Fan Avocado Salad)
— • • • • —

6 avocados, chilled, peeled and halved lengthwise
6 cups torn salad greens
24 strips roasted red peppers (either fresh or purchased) *
1 teaspoon Dijon mustard
1/4 cup wine vinegar
1 tsp salt
1/2 teaspoon pepper
3/4 cup canola oil

Whisk mustard, vinegar, salt and pepper. Gradually whisk in oil until combined.

Place each avocado half cut side down and slice it lengthwise in 1/4 inch cuts. Put 1/2 cup greens on each plate. On top of the greens, place each avocado half and spread it as you would a fan. Top each avocado fan with a cross of 2 pepper strips. Pour a small amount of dressing over each salad.

* See side note on page 6 for tips on roasting peppers.

Haricots Verts
— • • • • —

1 pound green beans
1/2 to 1 stick butter
2 cloves garlic, minced
Salt and pepper to taste

Sauté beans in butter and garlic until slightly tender. Salt and pepper to taste.

Haricots verts are those wonderful pencil-thin green beans that are hard to find but worth the effort.

Sea Bass En Croûte with Shallot Hollandaise

12 fresh sea bass filets (6 ounces each)
Olive oil, tarragon, thyme, chives, salt and pepper

Shallot Hollandaise Sauce
6 shallots, minced
3/4 cup red wine vinegar
6 egg yolks
1/4 cup water
2 cups (4 sticks) butter, melted and clarified
1 tablespoon fresh chives, chopped
2 teaspoons tomato paste
2 teaspoons fresh tarragon, chopped
Salt and pepper to taste

3 boxes puff pastry (2 sheets per box), thawed until flexible
2 egg yolks, lightly beaten

Brush each filet with olive oil and generously sprinkle with salt and pepper. Sprinkle with tarragon, thyme, and chives. Place on a platter, cover and chill for up to 12 hours.

For sauce: Boil shallots in vinegar until vinegar is evaporated. Using a double boiler, whisk egg yolks until they are light and lemon colored. Stir in 2 tablespoons of the boiled shallots. Add butter in a slow and steady stream, whisking constantly until well blended. Stir in chives, tomato paste, and tarragon. Then add (to taste) all or part of remaining boiled shallots. Salt and pepper to taste.

For pastry: Divide each pastry sheet in half (all twelve halves will wrap each of the twelve fish filets). On a floured surface, roll each of the twelve sheets of pastry to 1/8 inch thickness and big enough to go around each filet. Place each filet on each pastry sheet and fold the sheet around the filet. Mold and seal the edges of each pastry together forming a fish shape with a tail. Cut off excess pastry and roll out to make fins and eyes and arrange on the pastry covered filet. With a knife, score the tail and fins and draw a mouth. You can also form scales with a pastry knife and further decorate the fish by making a rope out of the excess dough and outlining the fish. Brush pastry with egg yolk. Preheat oven to 450°, reduce to 350° and bake until is golden brown, about 30 minutes.

To serve: Place fish on top of sauce on plate and pass. You may prefer to make three large fish using three to four filets per pastry.

If sea bass is not available, you may substitute snapper.

Enjoy the French tradition of lingering over your food until well into the evening.

For a beautiful presentation, French sauces are very often served under the entree.

Crêpes De Fraises Royale
(Strawberry Crêpes)

•••••

Crêpe Batter
2-1/2 cups all purpose flour
1/2 teaspoon salt
1 teaspoon baking powder
4 teaspoons sugar
4 eggs
2 teaspoons vanilla, rum or brandy extract
1/4 cup light vegetable oil
4 cups milk
Water as required
Butter for cooking
Sweet sherry to brush on crepes

Filling
16 ounces cream cheese, softened
1/4 cup powdered sugar
1 tablespoon grated orange peel
1/2 cup orange juice
Sweet sherry

Topping
1-1/2 cups apricot preserves
1/4 cup sweet sherry
1/4 cup butter, melted
3 pints strawberries, hulled and sliced
1 cup sliced almonds
Sour cream

12 whole strawberries and mint sprigs for garnish

For crêpes: Sift flour, salt, baking powder, and sugar into a bowl. Make a well in the center. Beat the eggs with the extract, oil and milk. Gradually pour this into the well of the flour mixture, whisking until the mixture is a smooth, creamy consistency. Set aside for at least 30 minutes, then whisk in sufficient water to produce a batter the consistency of light cream. Heat a shallow crêpe or omelet pan and grease lightly with butter. Pour in 2 to 3 tablespoons of the batter and tilt the pan to coat the bottom, pouring off any excess batter. Cook over medium high heat until the underside is lightly brown. Carefully flip the crêpe and cook another minute. Repeat, adding more butter as needed. Stack the cooked crêpes, separating each with waxed paper.

For filling: Combine the cream cheese, powdered sugar, orange peel, and juice. Lightly brush one side of each crêpe with sweet sherry and then spoon about 2 tablespoons of filling across each crêpe. Roll up loosely and arrange in a single layer in a well greased, shallow baking dish.

For topping: Combine apricot preserves, sweet sherry and melted butter. Spoon sliced strawberries over the crêpes, then spoon the apricot mixture over the strawberries, and sprinkle the almonds on top.

To serve: Bake at 350° for 10 to 15 minutes. Place a crêpe on each serving dish and top with a spoonful of sour cream. Garnish with a fresh strawberry and mint sprig.

If desired, flambé the crêpes in baking dish by pouring a little brandy over the crêpes and ignite just before topping with the sour cream.

Serve a good quality French wine with this dinner.

To prepare ahead of time, cover and refrigerate. Bring to room temperature and bake uncovered.

NOTES:

HAPPINESS IS...SPRING FEVER

Walnut Camembert Paté

Drunken Prawns

Caramelized Vidalia Onion Soup with Roasted Shallots

Romaine and Pepper Medley with Cashews

Spring Gourmet Lamb Chops

Porcini Mushroom Risotto

Roasted Asparagus with Grapefruit Hollandaise

Spring Fruit Trifle

SERVES 12

Springtime in Atlanta — breathtaking — endless clouds of

white dogwood blossoms gently draping over mounds of jewel-toned azaleas.

Graceful flowering peach, cherry and pear trees greet us at every turn.

Celebrate the season by displaying flowering tree branches

or forced branches of forsythia and quince.

Choose long branches and arrange loosely so that conversation is easy

underneath this airy umbrella of blossoms.

Tuck placecards in tussie mussies (or miniature bird nests)

of forget-me-nots, Johnny jump-ups and herbs.

Walnut Camembert Paté

— •• • • •— —

8 ounces Camembert cheese, rind removed
8 ounces cream cheese, softened to room temperature
2 tablespoons fresh lime juice
1 tablespoon fresh lemon juice
1/2 cup finely chopped toasted walnuts
Toasted baguette slices and assorted crudités (such as endive
    and red bell pepper strips)

In food processor combine the Camembert with cream cheese and process until smooth. Add the lime and lemon juice; process until smooth. Transfer mixture to a bowl and stir in 4 tablespoons of the nuts. Season with salt and pepper to taste. Sprinkle with additional nuts. Serve with toasted baguette slices and assorted crudités.

Drunken Prawns

— •• • • •— —

48 jumbo prawns (shrimp)
6 tablespoons butter, melted
1 tablespoon lemon peel, finely grated
1 tablespoon orange peel, finely grated
1/2 cup fresh lemon juice
1/2 cup fresh orange juice
1/2 cup brandy
2 ounces Amaretto liqueur
2 cups heavy cream
1/2 teaspoon cayenne
Salt and white pepper to taste
Round orange slices for garnish

Shell and devein prawns (shrimp), leaving tail intact. Season to taste with salt, pepper and cayenne. Sauté in melted butter in a large skillet for 4 to 5 minutes. Remove from pan and set aside. Add the lemon and orange peel, lemon and orange juice, brandy, and Amaretto to the skillet and bring to a boil. Add the heavy cream and cook until slightly reduced and thick enough to coat the shrimp. Return the prawns to the skillet and cook until heated.

Place orange slice in center of each plate. Arrange the prawns, four to a plate, in a circular fashion with the tails pointing in. Cover with the sauce. Serve immediately.

"Spring hangs her infant blossoms on the trees, rock'd in the cradle of the Western breeze."

William Cowper

❦

Prawns are shrimp-like crustaceans 3 to 4 inches long.

Stop those tears –
cut onions near a
gas burner or
open flame to burn
off the sulfur
compound before
it irritates your
eyes.

*Vidalia onions are
a hybrid onion
grown in Vidalia,
Georgia. The are
milder onions
because of the soil
and climate of the
region. Georgia's
early spring
provides a young
harvest so the
onions never
develop a "bite."
They are a real
treat because they
have a short
season, from May
to July, and do not
store well due to
their high water
content.*

*Whether for sugar
or onions, the
process to
caramelize takes
patience, stirring
and a watchful
eye.*

Caramelized Vidalia Onion Soup
with Roasted Shallots

20 shallots, peeled
1-1/2 tablespoons olive oil
1 stick butter (unsalted)
4 pounds Vidalia onions, sliced thin (or other sweet onion)
3 tablespoons brown sugar
1 cup cream sherry
1-1/2 tablespoons fresh thyme
1-1/2 tablespoons fresh sage, chopped
4 cups chicken broth
1 quart light cream
3/4 to 1 teaspoon Tabasco sauce, or ground cayenne to taste
4 tablespoons chopped fresh parsley
3 to 4 tablespoons minced fresh thyme
Salt and white pepper
Additional parsley sprigs for garnish

Toss peeled shallots in bowl with the olive oil, and place them on large cookie sheet. Bake about 30 minutes at 375° until brown, turning occasionally.

Melt butter in large pot, and add onions and sugar. Cook over medium heat until onions caramelize, stirring often, for about 45 minutes.

Add the roasted shallots to the pot, with half of the sherry, the thyme and sage. Cook for about 5 minutes, stirring occasionally. Add the broth and simmer for about 30 minutes. Add the light cream and simmer until soup thickens. Add remaining sherry, fresh thyme, parsley, Tabasco or cayenne. Salt and pepper to taste. Serve hot and garnish with parsley.

Romaine and Pepper Medley with Cashews

3 heads romaine, rinsed, dried and broken into bite-size pieces
1 cup salted cashews, halved
1/2 cup thinly sliced sweet onion
1 yellow bell pepper, cut into strips
1 red bell pepper, cut into strips
1/4 cup balsamic vinegar
1 tablespoons Dijon mustard
Salt and pepper
Pinch of ground cumin
Pinch of ground cardamon
1/2 cup light olive oil

Combine vinegar, mustard, cumin, cardamon, oil, salt and pepper. Blend well.

Combine romaine, cashews, onion, red and yellow bell pepper. Just before serving, stir dressing again. Add to salad and toss lightly. Serve salad on individual plates, taking care to distribute ingredients evenly.

Spring Gourmet Lamb Chops

24 1-1/2 inch thick loin lamb chops
6 tablespoons fresh lemon juice
4 tablespoons honey
4 tablespoons pepper jelly
4 tablespoons red wine vinegar
2 tablespoons fresh oregano or 4 teaspoons dried and crumbled
1-1/2 tablespoons fresh rosemary or 2 teaspoons dried and crumbled
2 teaspoons Dijon mustard
2 teaspoons minced garlic
2 teaspoons coarse salt
1/4 cup olive oil
Fresh rosemary sprigs for garnish

Combine lemon juice, honey, pepper jelly, vinegar, oregano, rosemary, mustard, garlic and salt in a bowl. Slowly whisk in olive oil in thin stream.

Trim fat on lamb chops. Place lamb in shallow baking dish. Stir marinade, then pour over lamb, turning to coat both sides. Let stand at room temperature 2 hours or chill overnight, turning occasionally.

Preheat oven broiler. Arrange chops on broiler pan. Broil about 4 to 6 minutes per side for medium rare. Transfer lamb to platter and brush with marinade. Garnish with rosemary. Serve immediately.

Balsamic vinegar is manufactured around Moderna in Northern Italy. It is dark brown in color and has a rich mellow flavor that comes from aging the unfermented juice of white Trebbiano grapes in wooden casks for at least 5 years. Some of these vinegars are aged as long as 100 years or more, which makes them very costly.

❦

The pepper jelly marinade may also be used on pork and grilled.

❦

Tie several sprigs of fresh rosemary together with twine to form a basting brush. Baste meat with the rosemary brush; it will impart its flavor onto the meat.

Porcini Mushroom Risotto

—•●●•—

The secrets to success with risotto are purchasing Italian short-grain rice (Arborio), using unsalted homemade stock, buying the very best Parmesan cheese and stirring frequently.

3 ounces dried porcini mushrooms
1-1/2 sticks unsalted butter
3 bunches scallions or green onions, chopped
5 carrots, peeled and minced
3 cups Italian Arborio rice
3/4 cup dry white wine
6 cups beef stock or beef broth
1-1/2 pounds fresh assorted imported mushrooms, wiped and sliced
6 cloves garlic, minced
1 cup chopped fresh parsley
Salt and pepper to taste
3 cups freshly grated Parmesan cheese
1-1/2 cups heavy cream
3 eggs
Pinch ground nutmeg

Place porcini mushrooms in a small bowl, cover with hot water, and let stand 30 minutes. Drain and reserve liquid.

Melt 3/4 stick butter in large skillet. Add the scallions and carrots and sauté for 10 minutes. Add the rice to the vegetables and cook for 2 minutes, stirring constantly. Strain the porcini liquid, then pour it over the rice. Add the wine and enough broth to completely cover the rice. Stir frequently over low heat, adding more stock as needed, until the rice is tender but still firm, about 30 minutes.

While the rice is cooking, melt the remaining butter in a skillet, add the porcini and fresh mushrooms, and sauté for 10 minutes. Stir in the garlic and parsley and simmer uncovered 10 minutes. Season with the salt and pepper.

Preheat the oven to 350°. Butter a 9 x 12 baking dish. Spread half the rice in the bottom of the baking dish. Top with all the mushrooms. Sprinkle 1-1/2 cups of the Parmesan over the mushrooms and top with the remaining rice. Whisk the cream, eggs, and nutmeg together and pour evenly over the rice. Sprinkle with the remaining Parmesan.

Bake until the top is puffed and brown, about 30 minutes. Let cool a few minutes before serving.

Roasted Asparagus
with Grapefruit Hollandaise

2 pounds fresh thick asparagus
1/4 cup water
1/4 cup butter
3 egg yolks
1/2 cup butter
4 tablespoons fresh grapefruit juice
1 teaspoon freshly grated grapefruit peel
1/4 teaspoon salt
1/8 teaspoon cayenne
Paprika

Wash asparagus and break off stems. (Use a vegetable peeler to remove outside peeling from lower parts of stem.) The stalk will naturally break between the tender and tough part. Place in a baking dish sprayed with vegetable spray or lined with parchment paper. Roast in a preheated oven of 475° for 10 to 12 minutes, until tender and slightly brown. Roasted asparagus have a nutty flavor.

For Hollandaise: Melt butter in 1 quart glass bowl in microwave until it bubbles, about 45 seconds. Mix egg yolks and grapefruit juice and grated rind in blender, add yolk mixture to butter and cook in microwave on high for about 1-1/2 minutes, whisking every 20 seconds. Stir in salt and cayenne halfway through cooking time.

To serve: Pour the hollandaise sauce over the spears. Sprinkle each serving with paprika. Serve immediately.

Choose asparagus that have crisp stalks with tight, unopened tips. If you are not going to use right away, wrap ends in damp paper towels and refrigerate in a plastic bag.

"The world's favorite season is in the spring. All things are possible in May."

Edwin Way Peale

Spring Fruit Trifle

3 packages plain Lady Fingers

Custard
6 egg yolks
1/2 cup Grand Marnier liqueur
6 tablespoons sugar
Dash salt
1 cup whipping cream

Cake Toppings
6 teaspoons dark rum
6 tablespoons unsweetened pineapple juice
6 tablespoons cream of coconut
1 16-ounce jar seedless blackberry jam

Strawberry Sauce
3 pints strawberries, hulled
3/4 cup sugar
2 teaspoons fresh lemon juice
Dash of salt

Papaya Sauce
3 medium-sized ripe papayas
5 tablespoons sugar
Dash of salt
1 pint fresh berries for garnish

For Custard: In the top of a double boiler beat egg yolks and liqueur until combined. Stir in sugar and salt. Place over boiling water (upper pan should not touch water). Beat with an electric mixer on high speed for 10 minutes or until mixture thickens and mounds. Cool completely. Beat the whipping cream until soft peaks form. Fold cream into the cooled egg mixture. Chill until ready to use.

For Strawberry Sauce: Puree strawberries in a food processor with a steel blade. Stir in sugar, fresh lemon juice, and a dash of salt. Refrigerate until ready to use.

For Papaya Sauce: Peel papayas and remove pulp from the pit. Puree papaya in a food processor with the steel blade. Mix in sugar and dash salt. Refrigerate until ready to use.

To assemble the trifle, using a straight sided trifle bowl, pour about 1/2 cup strawberry sauce into a bowl, covering the bottom. Place a layer of Lady Fingers over strawberry sauce. Sprinkle two tablespoons of rum, 3 tablespoons of pineapple juice, and two tablespoons of cream of coconut over Lady Fingers. Spread one third of the jam and 1/2 cup of strawberry sauce over Lady Fingers. Top with one third of the whipped cream mixture.

Repeat layering, beginning with Lady Fingers, until bowl is full, and ending with whipped cream mixture. Cover and refrigerate for 6 to 8 hours before serving. Garnish with fresh berries. Serve with Papaya Sauce.

BUDDHA'S BIRTHDAY FEAST

Beef and Pork Satays with Peanut Sauce

Pattaya Scallops

Hot and Sour Prawn Soup

Green Papaya in Tomato Flower

Gaeng Kiow Wahn Gai

Thai Fried Noodles

"Som" Celebration Cups with Cointreau Sauce

Buddha's Lace Fans

SERVES 12

The cuisines of China and India are colorful threads woven into the tapestry
of Thai cooking. Over the years, we have enjoyed
trying exotic cuisines. We hope in this menu to have brought together
the special flavors of Thailand for you to enjoy.

Food carving occupies a special place in Palace cooking.
Creatively carved fruits and vegetables add an artistic touch to any dish.
A stunning centerpiece such as this can set the tone for lively dinner conversation.
Cut a long, narrow slit in the top of a large melon.
Exotic and colorful lilies, quince branches and palm leaves can be secured directly
into the flesh of the melon. The melon juice will keep them fresh.
Woven bamboo placemats set over a tapestry
or batik cloth will continue the theme.
Tuck a lily into each napkin and slip on a wooden napkin ring.
This is the perfect time to add a collection of elephants, Buddhas or
Oriental objects to your tablescape.

Beef and Pork Satays with Peanut Sauce

Marinade
l cup teriyaki sauce
1/4 cup fresh lime juice
4 cloves minced garlic
2-1/2 tablespoons minced fresh ginger
2 tablespoons brown sugar

Meat for satays cut into strips 3 inches long,
     1 inch wide, 1/4 inch thick
1-1/2 pounds pork tenderloin
1-1/2 pounds beef sirloin or tenderloin
24 to 36 skewers, soaked in water for 30 minutes

Peanut Sauce
3 tablespoons peanut oil
3/4 cup onion, finely chopped
3 cloves garlic, minced
1 tablespoon crushed red pepper flakes or to taste
1 teaspoon ground cumin
4 tablespoons freshly squeezed lime juice
1/3 cup soy sauce
1-1/2 cup creamy peanut butter
1/2 cup coconut milk (unsweetened)
1/3 cup chopped fresh cilantro (optional)
Lime slices and hibiscus flowers for garnish

Combine marinade ingredients in a shallow dish, stirring until sugar dissolves. Marinate meat strips in refrigerator for one hour. Remove meat from marinade and thread on separate skewers. Cover and chill. (May be prepared two hours ahead.)

For peanut sauce: Heat oil in a saucepan. Stir in onion, garlic, pepper flakes and cumin. Cook for about 10 minutes until aromatic, but not brown. Add lime juice, soy sauce, peanut butter and coconut milk, whisk until smooth. Cook for 5 to 7 minutes longer over low heat until hot. (May be prepared two days ahead. Cover and refrigerate.) Before serving, stir over medium heat until hot, thinning with water if necessary.

Grill the skewered meat over hot coals or gas grill approximately 10 to 12 minutes for the pork, and 6 to 7 minutes for the beef, turning once. Meat may be broiled indoors for 3 minutes per side or until desired doneness is reached.

To serve: Place 2 or 3 skewers on each small plate, garnish with lime and flowers, and serve with peanut sauce.

On a nice evening, this might be served on a deck or patio with cocktails. Beer is the preferred beverage in Thailand and Thai beer is now available worldwide.

Freeze raw meats partially for thin slicing.

All people smile in the same language.

Pattaya Scallops

48 medium-sized scallops
1/2 cup melted butter
6 tablespoons lime juice
4 cloves garlic, minced
3 tablespoons fresh ginger root, finely chopped
4 tablespoons shallots, chopped
3 tablespoons cilantro, chopped
Salt and white pepper to taste
Fresh cilantro sprigs for garnish

Combine all ingredients in a large bowl. Using scallop shells or individual ramekins, place 4 scallops in each container. Distribute seasoning mixture evenly among the 12 servings. Bake at 350° for approximately 10 minutes, until just cooked, being careful not to overcook. Serve hot, garnished with a sprig of cilantro.

Hot and Sour Prawn Soup

6 cups chicken broth
3 stalks lemon grass (or peel from one lemon)
3 kaffir lime leaves (or peel from one lime)
1-1/2 pounds large shrimp, peeled and deveined
6 small fresh Thai peppers, seeded
2 tablespoons ground coriander
5 tablespoons fresh lime juice
2 tablespoons fish sauce or to taste

Peel lemon grass and use only the soft center stems. Cut into 1/4 inch slices. Add lemon grass and lime leaves to chicken broth. Cover and boil for 5 minutes. Add shrimp and peppers, continue cooking until shrimp are done. Add remaining ingredients and let stand for 5 minutes. Check the seasoning, adding more fish sauce or lime juice (Break up the peppers to release more heat as required.) If you have used lemon and lime peel, remove from soup. The soup should be spicy-sour and a little salty. Serve hot.

Make your guests aware that the small peppers are very hot. Eat with care!

Green Papaya in Tomato Flower

• ● ● ●

3 cups green papaya (about 1-1/2 pounds)
1-1/2 cups green beans
7 fresh small whole green serrano chilies
6 garlic cloves
1/3 cup fresh lime juice
1-1/2 tablespoons brown sugar
4 tablespoons fish sauce
1 cup unsalted roasted peanuts, chopped
12 cherry tomatoes
12 medium tomatoes

Peel and seed green papaya. Cut papaya and green beans into matchsticks. Cut 12 cherry tomatoes into quarters. Set vegetables aside. Seed chilies using rubber gloves. Put chilies, garlic, lime juice, sugar and fish sauce in blender or food processor and blend well. Combine vegetables, peanuts and dressing no more than one hour before serving.

To serve: On individual plates, place a tomato that has been cut to resemble a flower (remove stem end, cut into 8 sections leaving attached at the bottom, and spread open flat) onto each plate. Spoon the papaya salad mixture into the tomato flower.

Green papaya is a vegetable found in oriental markets; this is not the fruit variety. Green papaya (Son Tam) can be purchased in international markets throughout the world.

The combination of sweet and hot makes this a popular dish, sometimes eaten with sticky rice.

Gaeng Kiow Wahn Gai
(Green Curry Chicken)

6 whole chicken breasts
6 chicken thighs
1/4 cup green curry paste (available in specialty
    or international markets) or to taste
6 cups coconut milk (about 3 cans)
10 small white aubergines (eggplants) cubed
6 tablespoons fish sauce
2 tablespoons palm or brown sugar
1 teaspoon salt
10 to 12 kaffir leaves, torn into pieces
    or lime peel if leaves are unavailable
6 fresh red chilies, seeded and halved
1/2 cup fresh basil leaves, chopped
4 cups raw white rice (Basmati or jasmine), cooked

Bone and skin the chicken breasts and thighs. Cut into large bite-sized pieces. Stir fry the pieces in a large skillet or wok in a small amount of oil for a few minutes until chicken is lightly browned. Add the curry paste and stir to coat chicken. Add the coconut milk, eggplant, fish sauce, sugar and about salt. Stir well to mix. Add lime leaves and hot chilies. Cook for 12 to 15 minutes, stirring occasionally to maintain a gentle active boil. Taste and adjust the seasonings with a little more fish sauce, sugar or curry paste. Garnish with chopped basil.

Serve in shallow bowls or on the dinner plate over steamed white rice. This may be served as a separate course or along with the noodle dish.

Coconut milk does not come from the inside of a green coconut, but rather is made from shredded coconut meat placed in boiling water and milk. Thick coconut milk is made from the first pressing or straining of the coconut meat and thin milk is made from the second pressing.

Fish sauce may be purchased in an oriental or international market and may be used much like a light soy sauce.

Thai Fried Noodles

Sauce
1 cup water
1/2 cup tamarind juice
1/3 cup brown sugar
1 tablespoon white soya sauce

1/2 cup peanut oil
1 pound raw shrimp, shelled and deveined
4 ounces firm tofu, diced
3 tablespoons preserved sweet white radish, chopped
3 tablespoons shallots, sliced
4 eggs
1 package cellophane noodles (1 ounce or 300 grams)
    soaked in cold water for 7 to 10 minutes and drained
1/2 cup chicken broth
1/3 sup unsalted roasted peanuts, chopped
4 green onion, sliced
1 pound fresh bean sprouts
2 tablespoons fish sauce

For sauce: Mix sauce ingredients in a pan and boil until reduced to about 2/3 cup. Set aside to cool.

Heat oil in a wok until very hot. Add shrimp and tofu; stir fry lightly for 1 minute. Add preserved radish and shallots, fry for one minute and break in the eggs. Stir fry for a minute, then add noodles and chicken broth. When noodles are soft (about 2 minutes), add the peanuts, green onions, bean sprouts and fish sauce. Add the cooled sauce, fry for 3 minutes and serve. Top with extra chopped peanuts, chopped green onions and garnish with lime slices.

Buddha's Lace Fans

1/2 cup plus 1 tablespoon flour
1/2 teaspoon ground ginger
1/4 cup light corn syrup
1/4 cup packed brown sugar
4 ounces butter
1 teaspoon brandy or vanilla

Line 2 cookie sheets with foil. Grease foil. Preheat oven to 350°.
Mix flour and ginger. Set aside. Combine syrup, brown sugar and butter in heavy sauce pan. Bring to a boil over medium heat, stirring constantly. Remove from heat and blend in flour mixture. Add brandy or vanilla.

Noodles are eaten daily in Thailand and noodle restaurants dot the roadsides and city streets.

Sticky rice is the "bread" of Thailand and the most delicious treat is sticky rice cooked in bamboo.

A Thai dish is a work of art whether in a home or in a restaurant. Be creative in your presentations.

Drop level teaspoon of dough onto cookie sheet, 4 to 5 inches apart. Bake for 5 to 6 minutes until golden. Cool about 1 minute before removing. Cookies are fragile and will break easily. Store in an airtight container until ready to serve.

Top each orange cup with a cookie fan. Pass the extra cookies.

"Som" Celebration Cups with Cointreau Sauce

6 large oranges, cut in half in a scallop design
2 cups grated coconut, toasted (or a purchased coconut ice cream)
1/2 gallon premium vanilla ice cream

Cointreau Sauce
2 tablespoons butter
1/2 cup packed brown sugar
2 cups orange juice and pulp
2 ounces Cointreau (or other orange liqueur)
Mint or lime leaves for garnish

Cut 6 oranges in half by fluting or scalloping the edges of each orange. Carefully remove the orange pulp and juice from each half, reserving in a bowl. Place the twelve decorative halves in a dish.

Toast 2 cups coconut in a shallow pan for approximately 10 minutes in a 350° oven. Stir midway and watch carefully so as not to burn. When toasty brown, remove from oven and allow to cool.

Soften the ice cream. In a large bowl, mix the ice cream with most of the toasted coconut, reserving about 1/4 cup coconut to sprinkle as a garnish. When mixed, work quickly to fill the orange cups. Sprinkle with remaining coconut and freeze immediately.

For sauce: Melt butter in a large skillet. Add sugar and stir until dissolved. Add orange, juice and pulp; and cook until bubbly and syrupy, stirring often. Add Cointreau, heat for one minute longer and keep hot.

To serve: Remove oranges from freezer 10 to 12 minutes before serving. Drizzle small amount of orange sauce over each orange and top with a Buddha's Lace Fans cookies. Garnish with mint or lime leaves.

Summer

CITY SLICKERS GO WEST

Glen's Margaritas

Spicy Salsa with Blue Corn Chips

Stuffed Poblano with Shrimp and Chèvre

Avocado Soup Teased with Tequila

Cactus Salad

Tombstone Tuna with Mango Relish

Santa Fé Saffron Rice

Coco Loco Flan

Skewered Fruit

SERVES 12

A festive evening is assured with

this lighthearted menu and setting.

Greet your guests with a frosty margarita

served in clunky hand-blown glasses.

Arrange the blue corn chips and salsa

in a large, flat basket lined with

a bright bandana.

A centerpiece of varying sizes and types of cacti

arranged in a low pottery container

filled with sand adds whimsical interest.

You might even plant a variety of tiny cacti

in miniature clay pots

and use as placecard holders.

Place red and green chili peppers

in the folds of brightly colored napkins,

add mariachi music and

get ready for a good time, partner!

Glen's Margaritas

12 ounces frozen limeade
12 ounces tequila
4 ounces Triple Sec
Crushed ice
Lime slices for garnish

In a blender, combine limeade, tequila and Triple Sec. Fill the container with crushed ice. Process until pulverized. Serve in salt-rimmed glasses with garnish with lime slice.

Variation: Instead of Triple Sec, use another orange-based liqueur such as Cointreau or Grand Marnier.

Spicy Salsa with Blue Corn Chips

4 large ripe tomatoes, peeled and chopped
l medium sweet purple onion, finely chopped
2 serrano chilies, chopped
2 garlic cloves, minced
2 tablespoons chopped cilantro
5 tablespoons fresh lime juice
2 tablespoons olive oil
Salt and freshly ground pepper
Pinch of sugar
Blue corn chips

Mix all ingredients. Taste for seasonings and serve chilled with chips. Makes approximately 3 cups.

Cilantro resembles parsley in appearance but has a very distinctive and unique flavor. Try cilantro several times before you make a decision since its flavor seems to grow on you.

Serrano chilies are skinny, only about one inch long and are hot enough to make you cry. Handle with care! They are worth the effort.

Chilies are widely used in Mexican food and can range from very hot to a mild, almost sweet flavor. Ancho is the dried form of the mild poblano chili. The poblano is similar in size and flavor to bell peppers and is blackish green when fresh. Italian frying peppers or green bell peppers are a suitable substitute. Many cooks use gloves while handling these especially hot varieties.

Stuffed Poblano with Shrimp and Chèvre

12 poblano chilies, roasted and peeled *

Filling
6 tablespoons butter
3/4 cup onion, chopped
1-1/2 pounds raw shrimp, shelled, deveined
    and cut into large pieces
3/4 cup small green onions, chopped
2 to 3 jalapeño chilies, seeded and minced, divided
3 8-ounce packages cream cheese, softened
1/4 cup minced fresh cilantro, divided
6 hard boiled eggs, chopped, divided
Salt and freshly ground pepper

Sauce
1-1/2 cups chicken broth
1-1/2 cups heavy cream
6 ounces Chèvre cheese
6 teaspoons fresh lime juice

Fresh cilantro leaves for garnish

Filling: Sauté onion in butter until translucent. Add chopped shrimp, green onions and 1/2 of the jalapeño chilies; continue cooking for 2 to 3 minutes until shrimp turns pink. Cool. In a food processor, blend cream cheese until smooth. Combine 1/2 of the chopped eggs and 1/2 of the cilantro with shrimp mixture and add processed cream cheese. Season to taste with salt and freshly ground pepper.

To prepare chilies: Remove stems and seeds from poblano chilies. Spoon shrimp mixture into each chili.

Bake filled chilies in 300° oven for 10 minutes until warm.

For sauce: Reduce broth on high heat setting until reduced to 3/4 cup. Add cream and bring to boil; reduce heat to simmer. Add Chèvre and remaining jalapeño and stir until smooth. Mix in remaining cilantro, chopped eggs and lime juice.

To serve: Spoon sauce over chilies and garnish with fresh cilantro leaves.

* See side note on page 6 for tips on roasting peppers.

Avocado Soup Teased with Tequila

6 small avocados, peeled and pitted
3 tablespoons olive oil
3 shallots, chopped
5 cups chicken stock or broth, chilled
2 cups light cream
2 tablespoons tequila
Seasoned salt and white pepper to taste
Freshly grated nutmeg or 1/4 teaspoon ground
1 large red pepper to make twelve pepper rings
12 sprigs fresh rosemary

Pureé avocados until smooth. Sauté the shallots in olive oil for 2 to 3 minutes (do not brown). Cool.

Combine the avocado pureé with the chilled chicken stock, cream, shallots and tequila. Whisk until smooth. Add seasoning to taste. Chill.

To serve: Slice red pepper into rings. Firmly stick rosemary sprig into ring so as to stand straight up. Float atop each serving.

Cactus Salad

Dressing
8 green onions, chopped
2 jalapeño or serrano chilies, stemmed
1/2 cup fresh cilantro, chopped (or to taste)
1-1/4 cups fresh lime juice
5 tablespoons olive oil
1 teaspoon salt
2 tablespoons sugar

Salad Ingredients
2 cups corn kernels
1 15-ounce can black beans, drained and rinsed
1 jicama, diced
2 red bell peppers, diced
1/2 cup Nopalitos (cactus), diced, if available (1 leaf)

Leaf lettuce
Lime slices, twisted

In a blender or food processor, blend dressing ingredients until smooth. Refrigerate. (May be prepared ahead.) Combine remaining ingredients; toss salad with enough dressing to taste. Refrigerate. Place lettuce leaves on individual plates and top with salad. Garnish with lime twists.

The wooden stems of the rosemary plant, soaked in water, may be used as skewers to flavor meat or vegetables.

Jicama (hee-kah-mah) is a crisp root vegetable that resembles a water chestnut in texture but tastes slightly sweeter. It is frequently served in Mexico as an appetizer; simply cut into sticks or slices and serve with fresh lime and salt.

The pads of the prickly pear cactus (Nopales) are widely used in Southwestern menus – either fresh or canned. Try them as dippers with a spicy salsa.

Tombstone Tuna with Mango Relish

Despite their resemblance, small green tomatillos are not a variety of tomato. Be sure to remove the papery husk. Enjoy their tart flavor fresh or roast them for a more mellow flavor.

If tomatillo skins are tough, put in boiling water for one minute, then plunge into cold water. Skins should come off easily.

Sauce
10 to 12 plum tomatoes
1 large onion, chopped
4 jalapeño chilies
6 garlic cloves
2 cups chicken broth
1/4 cup fresh cilantro, minced
2 tablespoons fresh lime juice
1 stick butter, quartered
Salt and freshly ground pepper

Spice Mix
3 tablespoons chili powder
2 tablespoons ground cumin
2 tablespoons brown sugar
1 tablespoon salt
1/2 to 1 teaspoons ground red pepper
1 teaspoon coriander
1 teaspoon ground cinnamon

12 6-ounce tuna steaks
Olive oil

Mango Relish
4 mangoes, finely chopped
1 cup tomatillos, finely chopped

Fresh cilantro sprigs

Sauce: Roast first four ingredients in 350° oven for about 45 minutes, turning occasionally.

Process roasted vegetables and the rendered juice until smooth. Combine with chicken broth and bring to boil. Reduce to low heat and add the cilantro, lime juice and butter. Season with salt and pepper. Set aside. (This may be prepared a day ahead and reheated.)

To prepare tuna: Mix all spices together. Sprinkle each side of tuna steak with small portion of spice mix. In large skillet, heat olive oil and cook approximately 2 minutes per side for medium-rare. (May be grilled.)

For relish: Combine chopped mangoes and tomatillos.

To serve: Spoon sauce onto each plate, top with tuna and garnish with mango relish and sprigs of fresh cilantro.

Santa Fé Saffron Rice

4 tablespoons butter
l large onion, chopped
2 garlic cloves, minced
2 cups uncooked long-grain rice
3 cups chicken broth
l/2 teaspoon saffron powder (dissolved in chicken broth)
2 bay leaves

Melt butter in large saucepan and add onion and garlic. Cook until the onion is transparent. Stir in rice. Bring chicken broth to boiling point and add bay leaves and rice mixture. Reduce heat, cover and simmer for 20 to 30 minutes. Remove bay leaves and serve.

NOTES:

Mexican Coffee

Coco-Loco Flan

Caramelized Sugar
3/4 cup white sugar

Custard
3-3/4 cups milk
5 eggs, separated
1-1/2 cups sugar
Dash of salt
1-1/2 tablespoons butter
1-1/2 teaspoons dark rum
1/2 cup grated coconut
1/4 cup grated, toasted coconut

Pour 1 tablespoon sugar in each of twelve ramekins. Place in 350° oven for 30 to 35 minutes, or until sugar is a rich, golden brown. Cool.

Scald milk. Whip egg whites until stiff; set aside. Beat egg yolks with sugar and dash of salt. Add milk to the egg mixture and mix well. Add the butter and rum and fold in the egg whites and grated coconut. Pour mixture into ramekins with hardened caramelized sugar. Place ramekins in a pan of water and bake for 45 minutes in a 325° oven. Sprinkle the toasted coconut over top and continue baking for 15 minutes or until knife inserted in center comes out clean. When cool, invert onto serving plate with Skewered Fruit.

Skewered Fruit

1 pineapple, cut into 1 inch wedges
4 oranges, peeled and sectioned
4 bananas, cut into 1/2 inch slices
1-1/2 cups sugar
1/2 to 1 teaspoon cinnamon
1/4 cup dark rum

Preheat broiler. Thread fruit onto 12 wooden skewers, alternating fruit. Combine sugar and cinnamon, sprinkle evenly over fruit. Place skewered fruit on flat sheet and broil briefly until browned. Drizzle liqueur over each and place alongside flan.

Mexican Coffee

Add 1 teaspoon ground cinnamon for each 12 cups of dark roast coffee. Piloncillo (brown sugar) may be added to the pot while brewing or served with the coffee.

Serve in clay mugs.

Used coffee grounds may be mixed into your flower bed to make soil more alkaline. Roses love it!

SUMMERTIME . . . WHEN THE COOKIN' IS EASY

Mozzarella and Garlic Bruschetta

Soft Shell Crabs Amandine

Chilled Asparagus Cream Soup

Tomato Basil Salad with Feta Cheese

Aw Shucks Salmon

Au Gratin Potatoes with Peppered Boursin

Lemon Chiffon Mousse with Walnut Date Crust

SERVES 12

Transform your table into an aromatic herb garden.

Topiaries of every variety are available, as are all potted sizes of thyme,

scented geraniums, mint and variegated sage, to name a few.

Plant herbs in clay pots of varying size (the older, the better), covering exposed dirt

with a lush moss. Place votives in miniature clay pots

and scatter throughout the arranged herbs.

Use majolica saucers as butter dishes or under wine bottles.

Tie oversized French jacquard napkins with raffia

and tuck a sprig of rosemary inside...

an earthy but elegant tablesetting.

Mozzarella and Garlic Bruschetta

— •◦●◦• —

1-1/2 pounds mixed greens such as spinach, romaine, arugula
    and escarole, cleaned, dried and coarsely chopped
3 to 4 green onions, thinly sliced
4 garlic cloves, finely chopped and mashed to a paste
1/2 teaspoon salt added to garlic paste
2 to 3 tablespoons olive oil
2/3 cup mozzarella, shredded
4 to 5 large Roma tomatoes or 3 medium vine ripened tomatoes,
    seeded and chopped
Salt and pepper to taste
1-1/2 long loaves of crusty bread
1/4 cup olive oil
Garlic salt

    Sauté and stir garlic paste in olive oil over low heat for one minute in large heavy skillet. Add green onions, greens, salt and pepper. Sauté over moderately high heat until tender, 2 to 3 minutes. Drain liquid and put in a bowl to cool. Add mozzarella and spread on toasts. Sprinkle with chopped tomatoes and serve.

    To makes toasts: Cut bread into 1/2 inch slices and broil until golden brown, approximately 1 to 1-1/2 minutes. (Toasts can be made a few days ahead and kept in an airtight container). Lightly brush with oil and sprinkle sparingly with garlic salt.

Bruschetta is all the rage in restaurants and homes across America. From Italy, where it is traditionally a workman's midday snack, it is a perfect appetizer for summer combined with all the robust flavors of vegetables from the garden.

Soft Shell Crabs Amandine

Deep fried does not mean more fat. In fact, if the oil is very hot and crabs (or other foods) are cooked crispy and are well drained, they may retain less fat than if sautéed.

Soft shell crabs are crustaceans that are sold after they molt and the new shells are still soft.

1-1/2 cups sliced almonds
6 tablespoons unsalted butter
12 soft shelled crabs
1 cup milk or light cream
2 eggs
Scant one teaspoon salt and pinch of Celebration Seasoning
    or cayenne pepper
Flour
1/4 cup olive oil
Lemon wedges for garnish

Melt 6 tablespoons butter in skillet. Add almonds and sauté until golden brown. Keep warm.

Beat eggs and add milk and seasonings. Dredge crabs lightly in flour, then in batter, and back in flour again. Sauté 6 crabs at a time in 2 tablespoons butter and 2 tablespoons olive oil over high heat turning occasionally until crisp and reddish brown, approximately 4 to 6 minutes. Drain crabs. Repeat with remaining 6 crabs.

To serve: Sprinkle with almond mixture and garnish with a lemon wedge.

Crabs may also be deep fried in very hot oil. Cook until golden brown and crispy.

Lemon Mustard Sauce (optional)

3/4 cup mayonnaise
Juice of 2 lemons
2 tablespoons Dijon mustard
2 teaspoons dry mustard
Salt and pepper to taste

Mix all ingredients.

To serve: Drizzle the rim of the plate with the Lemon Mustard Sauce in a zig-zag pattern.

Chilled Asparagus Cream Soup

3-1/2 pounds fresh asparagus
1/2 cup rice
1 chopped medium onion
2-1/2 tablespoons butter
1-1/2 to 2 cups light cream
9 cups chicken stock or broth
3 to 4 tablespoons freshly squeezed lemon juice
1/2 teaspoon nutmeg
1/4 teaspoon lemon pepper
1/2 to 1 teaspoon seasoned salt
1 to 2 teaspoons instant chicken bouillon for flavoring

In a large pot, steam asparagus until crisp-tender, approximately 2 to 3 minutes. Drain, run under cold water and drain again. Cut stalks into 1 inch pieces, reserve asparagus tips for garnish. Set aside.

In large saucepan, sauté rice and onion in butter until rice is opaque. Add 7-1/2 cups of stock and bring to boil. Reduce heat, cover and simmer for 30 minutes, or until rice is soft. Add asparagus stalks, nutmeg, salt and pepper and bring to a boil, cooking until asparagus is very soft, approximately 4 to 6 minutes.

Pureé soup in blender. You may want to strain through a sieve. Add lemon juice and refrigerate. (Can be prepared 24 hours ahead. Refrigerate asparagus tips separately.)

To serve: Blend light cream into soup. Thin to desired consistency with additional stock. Adjust seasonings to taste. Ladle soup in bowls and garnish with asparagus tips.

Gather flowers after the sun has evaporated the early morning dew.

This soup is also delicious served hot.

Asparagus is the young shoot of a spring perennial plant. Choose firm, green stalks. If tips are opening or look soggy, they will be stringy and taste bitter.

Tomato Basil Salad with Feta Cheese

1/2 cup olive oil
6 tablespoons balsamic vinegar
1 tablespoon garlic, minced
1/2 teaspoon English dry mustard
1-1/2 teaspoon Dijon mustard
1/4 to 1/2 teaspoon sugar
1/2 cup fresh basil, finely chopped
8 ounces crumbled feta cheese
8 large vine-ripened tomatoes, sliced
5 to 6 green peppers, sliced in rings
Salt and pepper to taste

In a small bowl whisk together oil, vinegar, garlic, mustards, sugar, salt and pepper. Attractively arrange tomatoes and peppers on plate. Top with basil and feta. Drizzle lightly with dressing.

Au Gratin Potatoes with Peppered Boursin

4-1/2 pounds red new potatoes, thinly sliced
1-1/2 packages peppered Boursin cheese (5 ounce package)
2-3/4 cups light cream
2 tablespoons butter
1/4 cup fresh chopped Italian parsley
Salt to taste

Preheat oven to 400°. Lightly butter large oblong baking dish. Over medium heat stir cheese, light cream and butter until mixture is smooth. Arrange half of potatoes in overlapping rows in dish. Season with salt and pour half of cheese mixture over potatoes. Repeat process and bake for 1 hour or until tender. May cover with foil first half hour, then remove for rest of baking time to lightly brown. Sprinkle with chopped Italian parsley.

Aw Shucks Salmon

12 6 to 8 ounce salmon filet (skinless)
12 ears corn (corn cob and silk removed)

Topping
2 sticks butter (softened)
8 chopped green onions
10 ounce frozen tiny peas
4 tablespoons fresh dill, chopped
4 carrots, grated
3 to 3-1/2 cups corn (cut off cobs)
2 tablespoons chopped parsley
Seasoned salt or Celebration Seasoning *

2 lemons, halved
Cherry tomatoes for garnish

For topping: Melt butter in large skillet or sauce pan and sauté onions, peas, dill, carrots and corn for one minute. Remove from heat and add parsley.

To prepare shuck: Slice down the middle from end to tip, carefully peeling shuck back to expose cob. Snap and break off cob at base and carefully remove silk from shuck.   Place salmon in shuck. Squeeze lemon juice and sprinkle Celebration Seasoning or seasoned salt on salmon and then spread 1/3 cup or more of topping mixture on each filet.   Close shuck and wrap in foil. Place on a hot outdoor grill with cover. Cook for 25 to 30 minutes, turning occasionally, until salmon is done. (May be baked in a 375° oven for the same length of time.) When serving, remove foil and open shuck to expose vegetables and salmon.

Garnish with lemon wedge and cherry tomatoes.

* See Celebration Seasoning, page 14, side note.

Corn, beans and peas will lose their sweetness as the sugar in their tissues turns to starch. Store them dry and unwashed in plastic bags in the refrigerator.

This is an incredibly easy dish to prepare and all it needs to complete the plate is a side dish of potatoes or rice. The presentation is artful without being fussy.

Lemon Chiffon Mousse
with Walnut Date Crust

Crust
1 cup all purpose flour
2/3 cup chopped pitted dates
2/3 cup chopped walnuts
1/3 cup unsalted butter, cut into small pieces
1/3 cup firmly packed dark brown sugar
1-1/4 teaspoons vanilla

Mousse
8 eggs, separated, room temperature
1 cup sugar, divided
1 cup fresh lemon juice
1 tablespoon grated lemon peel
1 tablespoon unflavored gelatin softened in 1-1/2 tablespoons water
1-1/2 cups whipping cream, beaten to firm peaks

Topping
1 cup chilled whipped cream
16 strawberries, halved
Fresh mint leaves

Crust: Preheat oven to 375°. Generously butter 9 x 13 pan. Combine all ingredients in processor and blend until crumbly. Press mixture into bottom of pan. Bake 8 to 10 minutes or until edges are light brown. Cool.

Mousse: Stir lemon juice, egg yolks, 1/2 cup sugar and lemon peel in double boiler, stirring until sugar dissolves. Continue stirring over simmering water until mixture thickens slightly, approximately 3 to 4 minutes. Remove from water, then stir in gelatin until dissolved. Let stand until cool but not set.

Beat egg whites in large bowl until soft peaks form, gradually adding 1/2 cup sugar. Gently fold egg whites into lemon mixture. Whip 1-1/2 cup whipping cream in separate bowl until soft peaks form. Gently fold into lemon mixture. Spread mousse into prepared crust. Cover and refrigerate at least 6 hours. (This can be prepared one day ahead).

To serve: Cut into squares and top with whipped cream. Garnish with strawberries and fresh mint leaves.

GEORGIA ON MY MIND

Angel Biscuits with Country Ham and Apple Butter

Fried Green Tomatoes with Crab and Parsley-Basil Pesto

Savannah Seafood Chowder

Red Cabbage, Apple and Roquefort Slaw

Peachy Chicken with Brandy Cream Sauce

Crispy Baked Mashed Potatoes

Bronzed Spinach with Mushrooms

Chocolate Peanut Chiffon Pie

SERVES 12

The mood is elegant but not necessarily formal.
Tuxedos give way to summer attire. This menu features many
of Georgia's specialties: seafood, country ham, peaches, fried green tomatoes
and peanuts.

In keeping with the mood of the evening, the centerpiece is appropriately simple.
Use a large antique blue and white bowl filled with Georgia peaches,
picked fresh from the trees. Allow some of the stems and leaves to remain
on the peaches for added interest. While not a typical centerpiece,
it will set the scheme for this summer meal and the peaches will exude a mild fragrance.
If you are fortunate enough to have blue hydrangeas in your garden,
place a small bouquet on either side of the bowl of peaches.
A collection of blue and white mismatched china would look lovely on white Venetian
placemats with blue French jacquard napkins.
In this often hot season, the blue and white theme will cool the evening and
Ray Charles singing "Georgia On My Mind"
in the background will warm your heart.

Angel Biscuits with Country Ham and Apple Butter

2-1/2 cups self-rising flour
3 tablespoons sugar
1/2 teaspoon baking soda
1/2 cup shortening
1 package dry yeast
1/8 cup warm water
1 cup buttermilk
1 pound center-cut country ham slices
1 small jar apple butter

Combine the dry ingredients. Cut in shortening until mixture resembles course meal. Dissolve yeast in warm water. Stir into the buttermilk. Stir the buttermilk mixture into the flour mixture. Mix well. (Dough may be covered and stored in the refrigerator for one week.)

Roll the dough onto a floured surface to 1/2 inch thickness. Cut small 1 inch circles from dough. Place on a greased cookie sheet and let rise approximately 30 minutes.

Bake at 450° for 12 minutes or until lightly browned. Do not overcook.

Cook country ham according to package directions being careful not to overcook.

When biscuits are done, slice the biscuits in half. Place a piece of country ham the size of the biscuit on the bottom half. Spread with apple butter. Replace the top half. Keep warm until ready to serve.

To serve: Pile a pyramid of tiny filled Angel Biscuits on your favorite serving plate. Tie a ribbon around several stems of small flowers and lay on the side of your serving plate.

Whether inherited from Grandmother or found in a flea market, fine old china is often the cornerstone of a table top collection. Build on the foundation with compatible new pieces, all with the elegance of the originals.

To keep butter from burning, add olive oil.

The best green
tomatoes to use
have a slight pink
coloring.

The cold seafood
on the hot
tomatoes is a
unique and
delicious food
sensation.

Fried Green Tomatoes
with Crab and Parsley-Basil Pesto

12 1/2-inch-thick green tomato slices (about 3 large green tomatoes)
1 cup all-purpose flour, seasoned with salt and pepper to taste,
     sifted into a shallow dish
2 eggs, beaten in a small bowl
1 cup corn meal spread into a shallow dish
8 ounces lump crab meat
2 tablespoons sour cream
2 medium ripe tomatoes, peeled, seeded and diced
3 tablespoons minced chives or green onion tops
Salt, pepper and cayenne to taste

Pesto
1 small bunch fresh basil
1/3 bunch fresh parsley
1/3 cup pecans
1/2 cup olive oil

Vegetable oil for frying

In the food processor, finely grind basil leaves, parsley, pecans and
olive oil until smooth. Set aside or refrigerate.

Bread each tomato slice by dipping it first into the flour, then into the
egg, then into the cornmeal. Set aside.

In a small bowl, combine the crab with the sour cream, chopped
tomato, chives, salt and peppers. Chill.

In a large skillet over medium-high heat, heat 1/4 inch vegetable oil
until hot. Fry the breaded tomato slices in the hot oil on both sides until
golden and the tomato is tender. Drain on a paper towel. Discard the oil
and use fresh oil in the skillet for each batch of tomatoes. This keeps the
breading from burning and giving the tomatoes a burned taste. Keep hot.

Place each tomato slice on a plate, top with 1 tablespoon or more of
crab mixture, and garnish with the pesto. Serve immediately.

Savannah Seafood Chowder

1 pound fresh salmon steak, cut into 1/2 inch pieces
1/2 pound fresh bay scallops
1 pound fresh large shrimp, peeled and deveined
1/2 medium fennel bulb with tops
5 cloves fresh garlic, minced
1/2 cup green onions, chopped
2 tablespoons butter
2 tablespoons all-purpose flour
2 cups milk
2 cups light cream
2 cups chicken broth
1/4 cup sherry
1/4 teaspoon salt (preferably sea salt)
1/4 teaspoon cayenne
2 cups fresh or frozen whole kernel white corn
Paprika

Remove green tops from fennel; cut into sprigs and reserve. Cut bulb into wedges, remove core and discard. Chop fennel wedges. In a large saucepan cook fennel, garlic and green onion in butter until tender. Stir in flour, milk, light cream, broth, salt and pepper. Cook, stirring constantly until bubbly. Add corn, salmon, scallops, shrimp and sherry. Cook and stir for 4 more minutes or until shrimp turns pink and salmon flakes easily.

Ladle soup into bowls and top with fennel tops. Sprinkle with paprika.

Red Cabbage, Apple and Roquefort Slaw

The combination of apples and Roquefort cheese compliment this red cabbage slaw.

3 cups Granny Smith apples, peeled and thinly sliced
1/2 cup freshly squeezed lemon juice
1 large head red cabbage, shredded
1 cup crumbled Roquefort cheese
1-1/4 cups chopped fresh parsley
1/3 cup grainy Dijon mustard
1-1/2 cups light mayonnaise
Boston lettuce leaves

Toss sliced apples in fresh lemon juice. Drain off any extra lemon juice. Mix the shredded cabbage, 3/4 cup parsley, and 3/4 cup Roquefort cheese. Whisk mustard and mayonnaise together in another bowl. Add to cabbage mixture and toss to coat thoroughly. Gently mix in apples. Add remaining parsley and cheese and toss.

Arrange lettuce leaves on salad plate. Spoon mixture onto lettuce leaves. Garnish top of salad with 4 apple slices.

Peachy Chicken with Brandy Cream Sauce

Chicken
12 8-ounce boneless, skinless chicken breasts
8 peaches, peeled, seeded and sliced into thin wedges
2/3 cup chopped pecans
1 ounce brandy
3/4 cup bread crumbs
Salt and freshly ground pepper
Paprika

Sauce
1 cup chicken broth
1 cup brandy
3 tablespoons fresh lemon juice
4 tablespoons unsalted butter
3 tablespoons olive oil
2/3 cup thinly sliced green onions, including green stems
2 medium garlic cloves, minced
2-1/2 cups light cream
1 tablespoon hot sauce

Topping
6 tablespoons finely chopped toasted pecans
6 tablespoons minced fresh parsley
4 tablespoons grated lemon peel

Preheat oven to 350°. Pound the breasts between sheets of wax paper until double in size. Form pounded chicken breasts into a square. Sprinkle breasts with salt and pepper to taste. Mix the peaches, pecans, brandy and bread crumbs. Divide filling among the chicken breasts; placing the filling in the center of each. Roll up like a jellyroll, folding edges over so that filling does not run out. Place seam side down in a 9 x 13-inch baking dish that has been sprayed with non-stick spray. Sprinkle with paprika to enhance browning. Bake at 350° for 30 to 40 minutes until done. Remove from oven and cool about 10 minutes so that it will slice easily.

While chicken is baking, combine broth, lemon juice, and brandy. Simmer about 10 minutes. Meanwhile, melt butter with oil. Add green onion and garlic. Sauté 3 minutes. Add brandy mixture. Boil 7 minutes or until reduced by one third. Add cream and boil for 7 more minutes or until reduced by half. Stir in the hot sauce. Set aside and keep warm. Combine toasted pecans, parsley, and lemon peel. Set aside.

To serve: Slice chicken breasts into 1-inch slices. Spoon sauce onto bottom of plate. Place three to four slices of chicken on top of the sauce. Top with nut mixture. Pass extra sauce at the table.

Firm peaches may be peeled with a sharp knife. Place ripe peaches in boiling water for 30 seconds, remove and place in ice water. The skins will slip off easily.

❧

While peaches come in many varieties, all are either categorized as Clingstone or Freestone. With Clingstone peaches, the fruit clings to the pit whereas the fruit of the Freestone separates easily from the pit.

Crispy Baked Mashed Potatoes

・•●•・

Crispy potato skins add just the right touch to the smooth texture of mashed potatoes. For an extra taste surprise, add 4 ounces of goat cheese to the potato mixture.

8 large russet potatoes
1-1/4 sticks butter
1/2 teaspoon white pepper
1 teaspoon salt
Dash of ground nutmeg
4 egg yolks, beaten
1/2 cup milk
5 tablespoons butter, melted
Fresh parsley

   Bake potatoes in 400° oven for 1 hour. Butter a large baking dish. Cut potatoes in half length-wise and scoop out. Reserve skins. Add butter and beat until smooth. Season to taste with salt, pepper and nutmeg. Beat in egg yolks, then milk. Spoon into buttered dish.
   Cut potato skin into 1/2 inch strips. Toss with 5 tablespoons butter and place on baking sheet. Sprinkle with seasoned salt. Bake skins at 400° for 10 minutes until skins are crisp. Remove from oven. Top potatoes with skins. When ready to serve, reheat at 350° approximately 20 minutes. Serve immediately. Garnish with fresh parsley.

Bronzed Spinach with Mushrooms

・•●•・

2-1/2 pounds fresh spinach leaves, washed and drained
4 tablespoons butter
2 tablespoons olive oil
1 tablespoon minced fresh garlic
1 pound fresh mushrooms, sliced
Parmesan cheese

   Heat butter and oil in large skillet until hot and lightly brown. Sauté garlic for 2 to 3 minutes or until golden, taking care not to burn. Add the spinach and "bronze" over medium to high heat until wilted, about 3 to 5 minutes. Toss in sliced mushrooms and cook an additional 2 minutes. Keep warm or serve immediately. Sprinkle each serving with freshly grated Parmesan cheese.

Chocolate Peanut Chiffon Pie

Chocolate Graham Cracker Crust
1-2/3 cups chocolate graham cracker crumbs
1/3 cups butter or margarine, melted

Peanut Butter Pie Filling
2 8-ounce packages light cream cheese, softened
1 cup sugar
1 cup creamy peanut butter
2 teaspoons vanilla extract
2 cups whipping cream

Topping
1 12-ounce package semi-sweet chocolate chips
1 tablespoon butter
1 cup whipping cream
2 tablespoons powdered sugar
1/3 cup chopped unsalted dry roasted peanuts
Chocolate shavings

Combine crumbs and butter, stirring well. Firmly press mixture evenly on bottom and 1 inch up sides of a 10-inch springform pan. Bake at 350° for 5 minutes. Cool.

Combine cream cheese and sugar; beat at medium speed of electric mixer until smooth. Add peanut butter and vanilla; beating well. Set aside.

Beat 2 cups of whipping cream until soft peaks form; fold into peanut butter mixture. Spoon into crust.

Melt chocolate chips in microwave with 1 tablespoon butter. Mix in enough water (approximately 1/4 cup) until spreading consistency. Pour over peanut butter filling.

For topping, beat remaining cup of whipping cream until soft peaks form; mix in the powdered sugar. Spread over chocolate mixture. Sprinkle with chopped peanuts and chocolate shavings. Using a vegetable peeler, shave pieces of a semi-sweet chocolate square for garnish. Chill.

This is a very rich dessert! Cut small wedges.

The lowly peanut was elevated in stature when Jimmy Carter, a Georgia peanut farmer, became President of the United States.

NOTES:

"SIMPLY" ELEGANT

Pass-the-Ratatouille

Gusto Shrimp Gazpacho

Baby Spinach Salad with Grilled Onions and Gorgonzola

Grilled Steaks with Bourbon Sauce

Mushroom Cheese Grits

Steamed Broccoli with Horseradish Cream

Berry Peachy Pockets

SERVES 12

Midsummer in Atlanta frequently finds temperatures rising — and cooks seeking easy recipes to enable them to spend less time in the kitchen.

Consider serving this menu on an outdoor veranda or porch on a cool evening.

Enlist a couple of talented fellows to man the charcoal grill and invite your guests to dress casually.

In keeping with the casual theme, the table setting is especially lighthearted.

Fill a latticed basket with a cloud of loosely arranged perennials.

Nestle a miniature moss covered (just hot glue it on) clay pot alongside each placesetting. Use these as placecard holders, naming each guest a flower (Ginger - Ginger Lily, John - Johnny Jump-ups, etc.).

Place clunky pillar candles in larger mossed pots and tie with raffia.

The original seating arrangement may be changed after the salad and after the entrée, giving the flexibility to move outdoors and enjoy the barbecuing. A "Simply" Elegant evening!

Pass-The-Ratatouille

2 tablespoons extra virgin olive oil
4 large garlic cloves, chopped
1 large eggplant, unpeeled and diced
2 green bell peppers, diced
2 large tomatoes, chopped
1 onion, peeled and cut into one inch pieces
1 large zucchini, cut into 1/2 inch pieces
1/2 cup chopped fresh basil
2 tablespoons white wine vinegar
4 ounces Muenster cheese, grated
Salt and pepper to taste

Bagle chips or sliced baguettes

All chopping may be done hours ahead. Heat oil over medium heat in heavy pot. Stir in garlic and cook one minute. Add all vegetables and basil. Sauté for 5 minutes. Cover and simmer until tender, about 25 minutes, stirring occasionally. Uncover pot and let simmer until juices thicken, abut 10 minutes. Mix in vinegar, season with salt and pepper. (May be prepared up to two days ahead of time and refrigerated until needed.)

Preheat oven to 350°. Spread ratatouille in an attractive baking dish. Sprinkle with cheese. Bake until hot and cheese melts, about 15 minutes. Serve with bagel chips or sliced baguettes.

"There is no love sincerer than the love of food."

George Bernard Shaw

Ratatouille (ra-ta-too-ee), a savory mixture of eggplant, squash and tomatoes, is of Mediterranean origin.

This appetizer may also be used as a side dish.

Gusto Shrimp Gazpacho

*Chill cream cheese
in freezer to make
it easier to cut into
cubes.*

*Squeeze lemon
juice on cut
avocado to prevent
browning.
If mashing
avocado, placing
pit in center of
mashed avocado
to stop browning.*

1-3/4 pounds small shrimp, peeled and cooked (set aside 12 for garnish)
1 quart tomato juice
1 11-ounce can of lightly spicy V8 juice
4 large vine ripened tomatoes, peeled and chopped, retaining juice
7 green onions, chopped
2 cucumbers, seeded, peeled and chopped
2 stalks celery, chopped
1 garlic clove, minced
1/4 cup lemon juice
1/2 to 1 teaspoon Worcestershire sauce
1/2 teaspoon Celebration Seasoning *
2 tablespoons sugar
Salt and pepper to taste
2 ripe avocados, peeled and chopped
1 8-ounce package cream cheese, cut into 1/2 inch cubes

Combine all ingredients except cream cheese in large bowl and cover. Chill for at least two hours.

To serve: Stir cream cheese into soup mixture. Ladle soup into bowls and garnish with avocado and shrimp.

* See Celebration Seasoning, page 14, side note.

Baby Spinach Salad
with Grilled Onions and Gorgonzola

• • • •

3/4 cup olive oil
1/3 cup red wine vinegar
Salt and freshly ground black pepper

12 to 16 ounces baby spinach leaves
3 large Vidalia onions, cut into 1/2 inch thick slices
1-1/4 cups crumbled Gorgonzola cheese (approximately 1/2 pound)
3/4 cup toasted sesame seeds
1 to 2 teaspoons butter

Whisk together oil, vinegar, salt and pepper. Refrigerate.

Toast sesame seeds in small skillet with a little butter until seeds brown and begin to "pop," stirring constantly. Set aside.

Arrange onion slices in a barbecue hinged rack. Brush with olive oil. Over hot coals or gas grill, cook onions, turning occasionally until soft and browned. You may drizzle additional olive oil over the onions during cooking. Remove from rack and keep warm.

To serve: Distribute chilled and washed spinach leaves on 12 salad plates. Separate onion slices and arrange over spinach. Top with crumbled Gorgonzola and toasted sesame seeds. Drizzle vinaigrette over salads.

You may substitute roasted onions for the grilled ones in this recipe. To roast, arrange onion slices in a greased roasting pan, drizzle lightly with olive oil. Bake at 475° for approximately 10 minutes until slightly charred. Discard outer skins.

The key to storing Vidalia onions is to keep them cool, dry and separate. They can be stored in the refrigerator, or wrapped separately in foil.

Grilled Steaks with Bourbon Sauce

Salting beef before grilling sometimes toughens or dries out meat.

In grilling, choose steaks about 1-1/2 inches thick, trim external fat and make sure the meat is at room temperature. The grill should be hot (about 500°) with the rack close to the coals. For full flavor and tenderness, beef should be cooked rare or medium-rare. Cook the steaks 4 to 5 minutes per side with the lid down, or 3 to 4 minutes extra if a lid is not used. The meat can be rotated 90° to create crosshatching.

12 filet mignon or rib-eye steaks, approximately 1 to 1-1/2 inches thick
Olive oil
Freshly cracked pepper
6 tablespoons butter
2 large Vidalia onions, thinly sliced
3/4 cup balsamic vinegar
2-1/2 cups chicken broth
2-1/2 cups beef broth
6 tablespoons bourbon
Salt

Rub steaks with oil and season with pepper. Grill steaks 4 to 6 inches over hot charcoal. Turn once or twice until well browned outside but pink and juicy inside, about 8 to 12 minutes for medium rare.

In a large, heavy saucepan, melt butter and sauté onions until transparent. Add vinegar, broths, and bring to a boil. Continue cooking on medium heat until sauce thickens, approximately 15 minutes. (Sauce may be made in advance and refrigerated.)

To serve: Warm sauce thoroughly and add bourbon. Sprinkle each steak with salt and cover with bourbon sauce. Remaining sauce may be placed on table for additional serving.

Mushroom Cheese Grits

6 tablespoons butter
l cup onion, chopped
l-l/4 pounds mixed wild mushrooms, such as portabello,
    crimini or shiitake, sliced
9 cups water
2-1/4 cups quick cook grits
6 ounces Romano cheese, grated
6 ounces cheddar cheese, grated
Salt and freshly ground pepper

In a large saucepan, sauté onions and mushrooms in melted butter. Add water and bring to boil. Gradually add grits, stirring constantly with wire whisk. Reduce heat to medium and continue cooking 7 to 10 minutes until thickened. Set aside and stir in cheeses. Season to taste with salt and pepper.

Steamed Broccoli with Horseradish Cream

2 large bunches fresh broccoli
1-1/2 cups sour cream
1 tablespoon horseradish
1-1/2 teaspoons Dijon mustard
1/2 teaspoon salt
Paprika

Cut each broccoli flower into 4 to 5 inch long pieces. Cut each piece in half lengthwise. Arrange broccoli in large microwave safe dish and add 3 tablespoons water. Cover with plastic wrap and steam for 7 to 8 minutes or until stalks are tender. Allow to stand for a few minutes; remove plastic wrap and drain.

Combine sour cream, mustard, horseradish and salt in saucepan or microwave safe bowl. Heat thoroughly, stirring often.

To serve: Place a broccoli spear or two on each plate and spoon hot sauce on each, sprinkle with paprika.

Try these grits served in a roasted poblano pepper.

MUSHROOMS:

Champignons de Paris*: white, cultivated, crisp, pale and widely grown.*
Cremini*: the brown version of the cultivated white mushroom.*
Shiitake*: strong woodsy flavor. Stems are tough and should be removed. Store stems for use in the stockpot. Shiitakes absorb water like a sponge, do not soak.*
Portabello*: a fully developed cremini with more flavor. Good for stuffing and grilling.*
Enoki*: skinny stemmed with a crunchy texture and fruity taste. Use raw or heated.*
Cleaning*: remove stems level with caps, wipe clean with a damp paper towel. If they are especially dirty, plunge into cold water, swirl, lift and drain. Store in a paper bag in the refrigerator for 3 days.*

Berry Peachy Pockets

2 boxes prepared pie crusts or puff pastry
1 egg yolk, beaten

Filling
6 medium peaches, peeled and cut into small pieces
1/2 pint raspberries
1/2 pint blueberries
1/2 pint blackberries
1 tablespoon Kirsh or Framboise liqueur
1 tablespoon fresh lemon juice
1/3 cup sugar
3 tablespoons flour
1/4 cup butter

Glaze
1 egg white, beaten
2 tablespoons sugar
1/2 teaspoon cinnamon

Topping
1 quart vanilla bean ice cream
Powdered sugar
Mint leaves for garnish

Using a 5 inch saucer as a guide, on lightly floured surface, cut pastry into 12 circles. Brush each circle with beaten egg yolk. Place on greased cookie sheets.

In bowl, toss fruit with liqueur, lemon juice and all but 2 tablespoons sugar and 1 tablespoon flour. Combine remaining sugar and flour in separate bowl and sprinkle over circles, leaving 1 inch edge uncovered. Arrange fruit mixture evenly on center of circles. Pull pastry up and around fruit, leaving the center open. (It's meant to look ragged and interesting.) Brush outside surface with beaten egg white and sprinkle with mixture of 2 tablespoons sugar and 1/2 teaspoon cinnamon. Dot each pocket with 1 teaspoon butter. Bake at 400° for 15 minutes on top shelf of oven or until crust is brown and crusty. Serve warm topped with ice cream on dessert plates that have been lightly dusted with powdered sugar. Garnish each with sprigs of mint.

Harvest

AFTER THE HUNT

Hot Sausage Packages

Sautéed Portabello Mushrooms with Mussels

Pumpkin Soup in a Pumpkin

Pears and Walnuts over Chilled Greens "A La Daniel"

Quail with Apple Brandy Cream Sauce

Couscous with Sautéed Vegetables

*Chocolate Pecan Bourbon Cake
with Bittersweet Glaze and Raspberry Coulis*

SERVES 12

In the South, hunting has always been a tradition.

A feast of rabbit, quail or venison is enjoyed as a seasonal event.

We think there is something quite extraordinary about sitting down

in black tie surrounded by your best table setting to feast on fresh game.

If the hunters come home empty-handed,

remember farm-fed game is always available at your local market.

Autumn in Atlanta brings a bounty of inspiration for your table.

In this season, some of the best sources for centerpieces and dried arrangements

can be found right outside your door. To set the mood for this fall setting,

hollow out a large pumpkin and fill it with chrysanthemums,

branches of colorful fall leaves, wheat, oats or dried wild flowers

from the roadside with wild grape vine trailing over the sides of the pumpkin.

Spray miniature pumpkins gold and use at each place.

Write the guest's name on the side or attach to the stem.

Sprinkle fall leaves that have been sprayed gold on the table.

Brass chargers under your favorite dinnerware will complete the fall theme.

Hot Sausage Packages

Filling
1/2 pound hot Italian sausage
l clove garlic, minced
1 small onion, finely chopped
1 tablespoon unsalted butter
2/3 pound finely chopped mushrooms
1/4 cup fresh chopped parsley
3 ounces cream cheese, softened

Pastry
4 sheets of phyllo dough
1/3 cup melted butter
2 tablespoon fresh bread crumbs

Ribbons
6 green onion tops

Remove casing from sausage links. In skillet cook sausage, stirring until cooked through and browned. Remove and drain on paper towels. In same skillet, cook onion and garlic in butter over low heat until onion is softened. Add mushrooms and cook over moderate heat, stirring until liquid evaporates. Transfer mixture to a bowl, add sausage, parsley, cream cheese, salt and pepper to taste. Cool.

Working quickly, put one sheet of phyllo on work surface, brush lightly with butter and sprinkle with 1 tablespoon bread crumbs. Place another sheet of phyllo on top of first sheet and brush with butter. Cut sheets into thirds lengthwise and into quarters crosswise to form 12 squares. Put a rounded teaspoon of filling in each square, gather corners of phyllo and twist gently to seal. Continue making in same manner with remaining phyllo, butter, crumbs and filling.

For ribbons: Cut each green onion top into 4 thin strips. Place in a bowl and pour l/2 cup boiling water over to wilt. Tie each package in a knot with a green onion ribbon.

Bake packages on jelly roll pan in a preheated 400° oven for 10 minutes or until golden brown.

Go to your favorite butcher for fresh Italian sausage.

❧

For a nice presentation, serve packages on a tray covered with paper fall leaves purchased at a party or craft store.

Sautéed Portabello Mushrooms with Mussels

36 mussels
1/2 cup dry white wine
12 portabello mushrooms
12 button mushrooms
5 tablespoons butter
1 tablespoon olive oil
4 tablespoons parsley, minced
2 large garlic cloves, minced
4 tablespoons shallots, minced
4 drops of tabasco
Salt and freshly ground pepper to taste
3/4 cup fresh bread crumbs
3 tablespoons fresh grated Parmesan cheese
12 thin lemon slices
Minced parsley for garnish

Scrub mussels. Steam in white wine until shells open, about 5 minutes. Shell mussels and set aside. Remove stems from portabello mushrooms and chop stems finely along with 12 button mushrooms. (May be done in the food processor.) Melt 3 tablespoons butter in skillet and add chopped mushrooms, shallots, parsley, garlic, salt, pepper and tabasco. Sauté briefly until tender and set aside. Slice portabello mushrooms in 3 or 4 even slices. Brown in 2 tablespoons butter and 1 tablespoon olive oil. Turn and brown on the other side. Remove mushrooms carefully and place 3 slices of mushroom to form a fan on a cookie sheet, making 12 fans. Top each of the fans with 2 tablespoons of the sautéed mushroom mixture and 3 mussels. Sprinkle with bread crumbs and drizzle with butter. Brown quickly under the broiler.

May be assembled ahead. At serving time bake for 5 minutes at 375° and broil to brown.

To serve: Place fans on individual plates. Sprinkle each plate with minced parsley and garnish with lemon slices. Serve immediately.

Pumpkin Soup in a Pumpkin

••••

1 medium pumpkin
1 cup onion, finely chopped
3 carrots, finely chopped
3 stalks celery, finely chopped
2/3 cup butter
1 teaspoon salt
1/8 teaspoon nutmeg
1/8 teaspoon pepper
Pinch of allspice
2 bay leaves
2 teaspoon fresh thyme leaves
1-1/2 cups grated Swiss cheese
6 cups chicken broth
2/3 cup bread crumbs, dried in oven at 300° for 15 minutes.
1/2 cup white wine or dry sherry
1 pint light cream
Swiss cheese, grated for garnish
Fresh parsley, chopped for garnish

Prepare pumpkin by cutting a 6 inch hole in the top. Set top aside. Clean inside and remove seeds. Scoop out pumpkin flesh leaving 1/2 inch of pumpkin inside. Chop fresh pumpkin and cook with 1 cup water until very soft, about 20 to 30 minutes. Drain and mash to make 3 cups of pumpkin purée.

Sauté onion, celery and carrots in butter until tender. Add remaining ingredients including bread crumbs and puréed pumpkin. Pour into pumpkin and cover with top. Place in a pan or clear dish with sides and cook at 350° for 1-1/2 to 2 hours or until pumpkin softens and inside is bubbly. Cover with foil if pumpkin is browning. Remove bay leaves and garnish top of soup with chopped parsley and additional grated Swiss cheese.

Extra cooked pumpkin can be saved for later use in muffins, breads or cakes. Toast the seeds for garnishing salads or snacking.

To toast pumpkin seeds: rinse and dry seeds. Toss with a small amount of oil and spread on a baking sheet. Sprinkle with salt and bake for 25 minutes, stirring often.

Pears and Walnuts
over Chilled Greens "A La Daniel"

Dressing
3 shallots
1-1/2 cups olive oil
3 tablespoons walnut oil
3 tablespoons balsamic vinegar
3 tablespoons Dijon mustard
1 tablespoon sugar
1/2 teaspoon salt
Freshly ground pepper

Salad
3 tablespoons walnut oil
1-1/4 cups walnut pieces
3 large firm but ripe Barlett pears unpeeled, halved lengthwise and cored
10 cups torn mixed greens (watercress, endive, leaf lettuce, arugula)

Insert steel blade in food processor. With machine running, drop shallots through feed tube and mince, add remaining dressing ingredients and mix 10 seconds. Set aside.

Heat walnut oil in skillet and add walnuts. Sauté until lightly browned, stirring 4 minutes. Cool. Cut each pear half lengthwise into 1/4 inch thick slices. Put in bowl and pour dressing over. Cover and chill 2 hours.

To serve: Divide mixed greens onto plates and arrange 3 or 4 pear slices atop each plate, overlapping slightly. Drizzle with dressing and sprinkle with walnuts.

Quail with Apple Brandy Cream Sauce

18 quail
1 cup flour seasoned with salt and pepper
8 tablespoons butter
8 tablespoons olive oil

Marinade
1 cup apple brandy
1 cup apple cider
2 tablespoons balsamic vinegar
1 teaspoon fresh rosemary, chopped

Sauce
4 tablespoons butter
5 shallots, chopped
6 apples, peeled, cored and sliced
3/4 cup apple brandy
1-3/4 cup chicken broth
1/4 cup apple cider
1/2 cup heavy cream, warmed
Bouquet garni (consisting of fresh herbs such as rosemary,
    bay leaf, parsley, thyme and pinch of tarragon, tied together)
Fresh thyme sprigs for garnish

Cut each quail in half and place in large baking dish. Combine marinade and pour over quail. Refrigerate for at least 4 hours. Drain and dry quail. Dust each quail with seasoned flour. Starting with 2 tablespoons butter and 2 tablespoons oil, sauté quail in large skillet with equal amounts of butter and oil, repeating until all quail are browned. Place in two large baking dishes and cover with foil. Bake in a 350° oven for 30 minutes while preparing sauce.

In same skillet, add 2 tablespoons butter and sauté apples until slightly brown, remove and set aside. Add 2 more tablespoons butter and sauté shallots. Deglaze skillet with chicken broth, scraping brown bits and add bouquet garni. Cover and cook for 15 minutes. Remove bouquet garni and add apples and cream. Heat sauce but do not boil. Remove quail from oven, pour warmed apple brandy over quail and carefully ignite. This much brandy will create a very large flame. Divide sauce onto 12 plates and place 3 quail halves atop sauce. Garnish with fresh thyme sprigs.

A bouquet garni is a neatly tied bundle of herbs which, without disintegrating into the dish, imparts all of its flavors and is easily removed after cooking. The usual elements are thyme, bay leaf, parsley and celery.

❦

Game birds, especially quail, take well to a bit of sweetness in their preparation. The quail derive flavor from the apple brandy and cider marinade.

❦

Applejack is American apple brandy made from hard cider. If using Applejack instead of Calvados, add a little extra brandy to the mixture.

Couscous with Sautéed Vegetables

2 packages quick cooking couscous
5-6 cups chicken broth
4 carrots, finely chopped
1 large red bell pepper, diced
1 cup chopped green onion
1 cup chopped toasted pecans
3/4 stick butter
Salt and pepper to taste

Follow directions for cooking couscous on the box, substituting chicken broth for water. Sauté the carrots in butter for 3 minutes. Add remaining ingredients and sauté for 3 to 4 minutes until tender crisp. Stir the vegetables into the couscous.

To serve: Use an ice cream scoop to form couscous on each plate.

The vegetables may be sautéed several hours in advance but the couscous is best steamed just prior to serving.

Couscous has its origins in North African cooking. There are many easy and delicious ways to prepare it.

Quick cooking couscous is an excellent product that makes the lengthy steaming and special equipment for traditional couscous unnecessary. Couscous may be served with any poultry, meat or game.

Chocolate Pecan Bourbon Cake
with Bittersweet Glaze and Raspberry Coulis

Cake
1-1/2 cups toasted pecans
1 cup unsalted butter
8 ounces bittersweet chocolate, chipped (best quality available)
1 cup sifted unsweetened cocoa powder
6 large eggs
1-1/2 cups sugar
1/4 cup bourbon

Glaze
1/2 cup heavy cream
1/4 cup unsalted butter
5 ounces bittersweet chocolate, chopped
5 ounces semi-sweet chocolate, chopped
1 cup toasted pecans, chopped

Raspberry Coulis
2 cups fresh or frozen raspberries, unsweetened and thawed
13 tablespoons sugar
1 tablespoon Framboise (black raspberry liqueur)

Garnish
Fresh raspberries

For cake: Preheat oven to 350°. Butter 10 inch diameter springform pan with 2 inch sides. Line bottom with parchment paper. Butter parchment paper and dust with flour. Finely chop pecans in food processor. Melt butter in heavy medium saucepan over low heat. Add chocolate and stir until melted and smooth. Stir in cocoa. Remove from heat. Whisk eggs and sugar until blended. Add chocolate mixture; stir to blend. Add bourbon and pecans. Pour batter into prepared pan. Bake until sides are set but middle section of cake still moves slightly when pan is shaken, about 40 minutes. Transfer to rack and cool completely.

For glaze: Bring cream and butter to simmer in saucepan. Add chocolate and stir until melted and smooth. Let stand until cool but still pourable, about 5 minutes.

Release pan sides from cake. Turn cake out onto 9 inch cardboard round and peel off parchment. Set cake with cardboard on a rack. Pour glaze, covering top and sides. Refrigerate until glaze is partially set but still sticky, about 10 minutes. Press chopped nuts onto sides of cake. Transfer cake to platter and refrigerate for about 6 hours or overnight.

For coulis: Purée raspberries in food processor or blender. Strain into a bowl to remove seeds. Stir in sugar and liqueur. Refrigerate until ready to use, about 1 hour.

To serve: Spoon raspberry coulis onto plates and top with a 1 inch slice of cake. Garnish with fresh berries and mint leaves, if desired.

Framboise is a delightful liqueur made from framboises, small, black raspberries with a delicious fruity taste.

❧

For many people, the first rule of any dessert is to be chocolate. Chocophiles will certainly enjoy this delectably rich dessert.

NOTES:

HARVEST CELEBRATION

Bayou Crawfish Mousse

Pasta Gloria

Cream of Apple Soup with Campazola Croûtons

Arugula and Crab Salad with Warm Sherry Vinaigrette

Rolled Loin of Pork Stuffed with Apricots and Pistachios

Soufflé of Sweet Potatoes and Gruyère

Zucchini Cups with Buttered Peas and Baby Squash

Pear William Puffs with Crème Anglaise

SERVES 12

Elegance and a sense of style don't necessarily mean expensive!

Creativity leads to tablesettings that are interesting

and reflect the personality of the host.

A collection of napkins can enhance a tablesetting and are easily handmade.

Oversized napkins are particularly attractive. Vintage fabrics are reappearing and

make wonderful table runners and napkins. Create your own still life by filling

a market basket or dough bowl to the brim with "fruits of the harvest" such as

miniature squash and gourds, eggplants, artichoke, pears, grapes and apples,

to name a few. Nestle a couple of bundles of asparagus

tied with raffia into the arrangement. Trailing vines of bittersweet

complete this strikingly handsome composition.

Bayou Crawfish Mousse

—● ● ● ●—

1 package unflavored gelatin
1/2 cup cold water
1/2 cup tomato juice
12 ounces light cream cheese, softened
1/4 cup light mayonnaise
2 tablespoons fresh lemon juice
1 tablespoon fresh chives, minced
1 tablespoon fresh parsley, minced
4 green onions, chopped, including some of green top
1/2 cup jicama, chopped
6 ounces crawfish tails cut into 3 or 4 pieces (may use frozen)
Salt, cayenne pepper and garlic powder
Dash of Tabasco sauce

Sauté crawfish for 3 to 4 minutes in a small amount of butter, seasoning very generously with salt, pepper, cayenne and garlic powder. Set aside.

In a medium saucepan, sprinkle gelatin over water; let stand for a couple of minutes. Add tomato juice and stir with wire whisk over medium heat until gelatin dissolves completely. In a food processor, process cream cheese, mayonnaise, tomato mixture, lemon juice, chives, and parsley until smooth. Stir in green onions, jicama, and crawfish. Adjust seasoning. Pour into greased 5 to 6 cup mold (a fish mold may be used). Chill for several hours or overnight.

To serve: Unmold by dipping mold in warm water for a few seconds to loosen. Turn onto tray and decorate attractively using sliced ripe olives, green onion tops and almond slices for garnish. Serve with toast points, crackers or bagel chips.

Decorate your mold by using olives for eyes and long slices of green onions on tail.

Sliced almonds make great fish scales.

Crawfish are gaining in popularity outside of Louisiana and the tails are usually available frozen in 8 ounce or 1 pound packages.

Pasta Gloria

• • • • •

1-1/4 pounds angel hair pasta, cooked

Sauce
4 tablespoons butter
3/4 cup shallots, minced
12 ounces shiitake mushrooms, sliced
4 tablespoons olive oil
1 8-ounce jar sun-dried tomatoes in oil, drained and sliced
    into thin strips
3/4 cup white wine
1 pint light cream
1/2 teaspoon cracked red pepper
Salt and freshly ground pepper
1/2 cup fresh basil, chopped
Freshly grated Parmesan cheese
Basil sprigs for garnish

In small skillet, sauté shallots briefly in butter, set aside. In large, heavy skillet, sauté mushrooms in olive oil. Add sun-dried tomatoes, sautéed shallots and cracked pepper, simmer briefly. Add wine and light cream and continue to simmer on low heat about 10 minutes until sauce thickens slightly. Season to taste with salt and pepper. Stir in fresh basil.

Gently toss with cooked pasta. Serve small individual portions. Grate fresh Parmesan over each and place a basil sprig on each plate for garnish.

To prepare pasta in advance, cook as directed (always al dente), drain and lightly toss with oil. Cover pasta with a damp cloth and refrigerate. Before serving, dip pasta briefly in boiling water.

Sun-dried tomatoes add wonderful flavor to salad dressings, pasta dishes and cheese spreads. They are available dried and in oil. If using dried, you may reconstitute in a little boiling water. Allow to absorb the liquid for about 15 minutes.

Reserve the oil from the jar of sun-dried tomatoes for use in salad dressings or for cooking. It imparts a delicious flavor.

Thinly sliced grilled chicken may be added to this pasta.

Cream of Apple Soup
with Campazola Croûtons

————— •◦●◦• —————

Soup
8 tablespoons butter (1 stick)
8 large Arkansas Black or other tart apples, peeled and sliced
3 onions, chopped
3 cloves garlic, minced
7 to 8 cups chicken broth
1/2 cup Applejack liqueur or 1/3 cup Calvados brandy
1 pint whipping cream
1/4 teaspoon cayenne
Salt and freshly ground white pepper

Campazola Croûtons
French baguette
6 ounces Campazola cheese or Saga Bleu
6 tablespoons softened butter
1/2 pound bacon, cooked, drained and crumbled

In a large, heavy saucepan, cook apples and onions in melted butter for 5 minutes. Add garlic and continue cooking for a few minutes longer. Stir in chicken broth and simmer until apples are soft. Season with cayenne and salt and pepper to taste. With a hand mixer, blend until smooth. (May be prepared and refrigerated for 1 to 2 days.)

Slice baguette into 1/2 inch rounds. Mix cheese and butter. Toast rounds on one side; turn to other side and spread with cheese mixture.

To serve: Reheat soup and add cream and liqueur. Broil croûtons until toasted. Ladle soup into individual bowls, place a croûton on each, and sprinkle with crumbled bacon. Additional croûtons may be served on each plate with soup.

Calvados comes from apples, especially grown in the Calvados region in Normandy, France. A well-aged Calvados exhales the very air of autumn. It has an intense apple flavor. Calvados works well in cream-based sauces. If substituting Applejack for Calvados, add a little brandy or cognac.

Arugula and Crab Salad with Warm Sherry Vinaigrette

Dressing
1-1/2 cups virgin olive oil
3/4 cup shallots, minced
3/4 cup Sherry wine vinegar
1-1/2 tablespoons Dijon mustard
Salt and freshly ground pepper

Salad
4 tablespoons virgin olive oil
2 red bell peppers (or 1 red and 1 yellow), thinly sliced
6 to 8 green onions, diced with most of green top included
1 pound crabmeat
10 to 12 cups arugula
3/4 cup fresh basil leaves, coarsely chopped

In a heavy saucepan, sauté shallots in 4 tablespoons oil until softened, approximately 3 to 4 minutes. Remove from heat and add vinegar, mustard, salt and pepper. Whisk in remaining olive oil. (May be prepared ahead.)

Heat 4 tablespoons oil in heavy pan and sauté peppers and green onions until just wilted. Stir in crab and continue cooking until just warmed. Remove from heat.

To serve: Warm vinaigrette in microwave. Lightly toss arugula with enough vinaigrette to lightly coat. Season with salt and pepper. Place greens on individual plates and top with crab mixture.

Sprinkle chopped basil leaves over each for garnish.

Rolled Loin of Pork Stuffed with Apricots and Pistachios

—••••—

2 4-pound boneless pork loin roasts, butterflied

Marinade
3 cups apple cider
3 cups dry white wine
3/4 cup cider vinegar
3/4 cup Applejack
l cup onion, chopped
6 garlic cloves, minced
5 cardamon pods, crushed
7 whole cloves
2 teaspoons ground ginger
1 tablespoon allspice, crushed
1-1/2 tablespoons coarsely ground pepper
Fresh sprigs of thyme for garnish.

Stuffing
6 tablespoons butter
2 cups green onion, chopped fine
1 onion, finely chopped
5 garlic cloves, minced
1-1/2 cups dried apricots, chopped
12 ounces pistachios
1/2 cup pine nuts, lightly toasted
1 cup fresh parsley, minced
2-1/2 tablespoons lemon peel, grated
1 tablespoon apple cider vinegar
Salt and freshly ground pepper

l to 2 days ahead, combine all marinade ingredients in large bowl. Marinate butterflied roasts in refrigerator, turning occasionally to coat.

To butterfly pork loin: cut top and bottom loin in half just to the long edge, without cutting completely through. Flatten to 1/2 inch thickness. (Most butchers will butterfly the roasts on request.)

Sauté onions and garlic in heavy skillet. Remove from heat. In a large bowl, combine the sautéed onion and garlic with the remaining stuffing ingredients. (May be prepared ahead and refrigerated.)

Preheat oven to 400°. Remove roast from marinade and pat dry. Strain and reserve marinade. Place each roast fat side down and spread 1/2 of the stuffing mixture over surface, leaving l inch from edges. Roll lengthwise and tie with string. Place roasts in deep roasting pan on rack with half of the marinade. Roast for 1 hour, basting frequently and generously with marinade in pan. Reduce heat to 350°. Continue basting frequently for about 1-1/4 hours or until meat registers between 150 to

Extra stock may be frozen in ice cube trays. When frozen, remove and store in plastic freezer bags. Great for sauces, soups and stews.

To flatten meat, pound between sheets on a strong paper with a meat mallet until the desired thickness is achieved.

If you "double butterfly," less flattening is necessary.

To "double butterfly," make a slit 1/3 of the way down, almost to the long edge. Turn over and repeat on the other side, slitting in opposite side. Spread open to about a 12 to 14 inch square. Flatten as necessary.

160°. Keep roasts warm. Degrease pan juices. Add remaining marinade and reduce juices until thickened. Season to taste.

To serve: Slice into 3/4 inch slices, keeping stuffing intact. Arrange attractively on plate and garnish with sprigs of thyme. Pass sauce at table.

Soufflé of Sweet Potatoes and Gruyère

1-1/2 cups onion, chopped
2 garlic cloves, minced
4 tablespoons flour
4 tablespoons butter
2 cups milk
2 cups Gruyère cheese, grated (approximately 6 ounces)
4 cups cooked sweet potatoes, mashed
8 eggs, separated
l cup freshly grated Parmesan cheese
Salt and freshly ground pepper

In a large saucepan, sauté onions in butter. Add the flour, stirring constantly until smooth. Whisk in the milk and simmer until mixture thickens. Remove from heat and add Gruyère, stirring until melted. Whisk in sweet potatoes and egg yolks, a couple at a time. In a large bowl, beat egg whites with electric mixer until stiff peaks form. Gently fold egg whites into potato mixture.

Butter two 1-1/2 quart soufflé dishes and dust with 1/2 cup (1/4 each) Parmesan. Pour potato mixture into soufflé dishes. Sprinkle 1/2 cup (1/4 each) Parmesan on top of soufflés. Preheat oven to 375°. Bake for approximately 45 minutes until puffed. Serve immediately.

Zucchini Cups with Buttered Peas and Baby Squash

4 very large zucchini
12 red pepper strips
12 miniature yellow squash
2 packages frozen tiny peas
3 tablespoons butter, melted
1/8 teaspoon garlic powder
1/3 teaspoon each of thyme, basil and dill
Salt and freshly ground pepper

Slice zucchini into 2 inch thick rounds. Scoop out center to form small cups. Blanch the zucchini rounds, pepper slices and squash and set aside. Blanch peas and drain. Add melted butter and spices to the peas. Lightly salt and pepper the zucchini rounds and fill with peas. Top each with peppers and a baby squash. Place filled rounds in a large baking dish. Cover with plastic wrap. When ready to serve, heat in microwave 3 to 5 minutes.

Pear William Puffs with Crème Anglaise

2 boxes frozen puff pastry (4 sheets)

Filling
3/4 cup butter
1/2 cup sugar
1-1/2 cups almonds, toasted and ground
2 eggs
3 teaspoons flour
3 tablespoons brandy
1-1/2 teaspoons almond extract
6 Anjou pears, peeled, cored and cut in half
4 tablespoons fresh lemon juice

Crème Sauce
2 cups light cream
2/3 cup sugar
6 egg yolks
4 tablespoons fruit brandy such as Poire Williams or Calvados
1-1/2 teaspoons vanilla

"The greatest calamity is not to have failed but to have failed to try."

Unknown

"Life is not the wick or the candle – it is the burning."

Unknown

Poire Williams is a pear liqueur that may be difficult to find and can be quite costly. Calvados is a reasonable substitute.

This dessert is not simple but the result is a delicious masterpiece.

Berry Sauce
1-1/2 pints fresh strawberries, stemmed and thinly sliced
2 tablespoons sugar
3 tablespoons Kirsch

Glaze
2 eggs, beaten with 1/4 cup heavy cream

To prepare pastry: Separate pastry sheets and cut 3 of the sheets into quarters. Place sheets on non-stick cookie sheets, leaving about 1 inch between each. Use fourth pastry sheet to make leaves or other autumn designs for decoration. Cover and set aside.

To prepare filling: Cream butter and sugar with electric mixer. Add almonds, eggs, flour, brandy and almond extract.

For crème sauce: In a large saucepan, scald cream. Blend egg yolks and sugar in a large bowl. Slowly stir in scalded half-and-half. Return mixture to saucepan and cook on medium heat until thickened, about 4 to 5 minutes. Cool. Stir in fruit brandy and vanilla. Cover and refrigerate. (May be prepared a day in advance.)

For berry sauce: In a food processor, puree strawberries with sugar, add Kirsch. In a saucepan, simmer over low heat until sugar is completely dissolved. Refrigerate. (May be prepared a day in advance.)

To assemble: Squeeze lemon juice over pear halves. With knife, enlarge opening in center of each pear half for filling. Place each pear half on pastry rectangle and pour a few tablespoons of filling mixture into indentation. Wrap pastry around pear half, moistening edges with water to seal completely. Turn pastry over, seam side down and decorate with pastry cut outs. Brush pastries with glaze and refrigerate for 1 hour. (May be prepared 3 to 4 hours in advance.)

To serve: Preheat oven to 400°. Glaze pastries and bake for 15 minutes. Reduce heat to 375° and continue baking until browned, about 15 minutes more. Cool slightly. Spoon small amount of each sauce on either side of each dessert plate. Place pastry in center.

FIESTA CON AMIGOS EN ESPAÑA

Tapas

Empañadas con Carne de Cordero

Champiñones al Ajillo

Sopa De Calabaza y Ajo

Ensalada de los Moros

Cocino Asado

Arroz Primavera con Azafran

Tarta de los Musicianos

Café Español

SERVES 12

We agree with the old Spanish proverb,
"He who has not seen Sevilla has not seen a wonder."
Some in our group have traveled to Spain and enjoyed the subtle,
refined and down-to-earth cuisine,
returning with memories of the Cocino Asado (served at the restaurant,
Sobrino de Botin) and wonderful tapas at local tascas in Madrid.
The food of Spain is not necessarily hot and spicy.
Spaniards enjoy it all, from churros and chocolate, to tapas and tartas.

We think this festive dinner calls for vibrant colors.
Use Picasso-like sunny yellows and bright reds for your flowers and tablecloth.
For the container, hollow out a combination of squash, eggplant and melon in lieu of
vases. Insert a glass container in each one to hold water.
Don't be afraid to enhance your floral arrangement with unusual ingredients
such as berries and seed heads to make an autumn statement.
Give each guest a Spanish name on their placecard such as Juan for John and
Margarita for Margaret. Softly play "Malagueña," "Bolero"
or "An Evening In Madrid" in the background.

Men love boutonnieres! This is a perfect evening to give each
a red or yellow blossom to wear.
As Mark Twain said, "Whatever a man's age,
he can reduce it several years
by putting a bright colored flower in his buttonhole."

Tapas

—•◦•◦•—

These two dishes are called "Tapas," which translated literally means "small bites" and are considered appetizers in Spain. An entire meal can be made of several "tapas," typical of which are fried squid (calamares), mussels, tripe, Tortilla Española (a potato omelette) and various cheeses with bread. A good vino tinto or a sangria is a great accompaniment.

Empañadas con Carne de Cordero
(Meat Pies with Curried Lamb)

—•◦•◦•—

Pastry
1 box frozen pastry sheets (2)
3 tablespoons curried oil

Curried Oil
1/2 cup vegetable oil
1-1/2 teaspoons ground curry powder
1/2 teaspoon cumin
1/4 teaspoon ground cloves
3/4 teaspoon tumeric
1/4 teaspoon white pepper
1/4 teaspoon coriander seeds
1 small clove garlic, sliced
1/2 teaspoon dried red pepper flakes

Lamb Filling
4 tablespoons light olive oil
4 cloves minced garlic
1 tablespoon fresh ginger, peeled and minced
1-1/2 cups minced onion
1 tablespoon jalapeño pepper, seeded and chopped
2 tablespoons ground cumin
1 teaspoon ground cloves
1 pound lamb, coarsely ground
3/4 cup pine nuts, toasted
1/4 cup dried figs, chopped
2 tablespoons fresh mint, chopped
1 tablespoon white pepper
Salt to taste

Glaze
2 egg yolks whisked with 2 tablespoons water

Fresh cilantro for garnish

Herb tip: Cilantro and Coriander are from the same plant. Cilantro, a leaf similar to parsley, is used in the fresh form as a garnish or added to recipes for its distinct flavor and Coriander, which is a seed. They have two totally different flavors. The dried powdered leaves are an additive in curry powder.

Extra curried oil compliments many lamb and chicken dishes.

"¡Buen Provecho!"

Enjoy your meal!

On floured board, form dough into two balls. Add 1-1/2 tablespoons curried oil to each ball of dough and work into the dough. Wrap in plastic wrap and refrigerate overnight or several hours.

To make meat filling, sauté garlic and ginger in olive oil in a large skillet until lightly brown. Add the onion and jalapeño and sauté another 3 to 5 minutes. Add remaining seasonings before adding the lamb, which will cook for about 15 minutes. Add pine nuts, figs and mint, mix well and adjust seasonings. Allow to cool before assembling with the pastry. (This may be done a day ahead of time and refrigerated.)

To assemble the empanadas, roll out one ball of pastry at a time on floured board to 1/8 inch thickness. Cut into 3 inch squares. Place a spoonful of lamb filling in center of each square. Brush edges with egg yolk glaze and fold over into triangles, sealing pastry with tines of a fork on the open sides.

Place on greased cookie sheet. (These may be made ahead of time and refrigerated or frozen until ready to bake.) Baste with egg yolk glaze, pierce with a fork and bake in preheated 400° oven for 15 to 18 minutes, or until golden brown. Serve warm as a "tapas" (appetizer) course, either passing around or seated at the table.

Champiñones al Ajillo
(Mushrooms in Garlic Sauce)

6 tablespoons olive oil
1 pound mushrooms
5 cloves garlic thinly sliced
4 teaspoons fresh lemon juice
4 tablespoons dry Spanish sherry
1/2 cup beef broth
1 teaspoon paprika
1/2 teaspoon crushed red pepper
Salt and freshly ground black pepper to taste
3 tablespoons minced parsley

Heat oil in skillet, and fry mushrooms and garlic over medium high heat for 2 minutes. Lower heat and stir in lemon juice, sherry, broth and all seasonings except parsley. Simmer for 2 minutes. (May be prepared ahead to this point.) Sprinkle with parsley and serve piping hot in individual ramekins with a toasted baguette slice.

Sopa de Calabaza y Ajo
(Garlic and Roasted Squash Soup)

Stock
1 large fryer, 3 to 3-1/2 pounds
2 carrots
3 stalks celery
3 quarts water

Soup
1 pound yellow squash
Olive oil
1 pound zucchini
Dried thyme
12 tablespoons (1-1/2 sticks) butter
6 green spring onions (scallions), thinly sliced
5 tablespoons minced fresh garlic
6 serrano chilies, thinly sliced, seeds and membranes removed
1 teaspoon fresh thyme
1 tablespoon fresh tarragon
1 tablespoon chopped fresh parsley
Salt and pepper to taste (preferably sea salt)
1/2 cup fresh mushrooms, sliced
10 cups chicken stock
2 cups fat free sour cream

Quarter chicken and place in a large stock pot. Add the carrots, celery and water, and cook for 1-1/2 hours until chicken is completely done. Remove the chicken from the stock. Discard the carrots and celery. (May be prepared ahead.)

Slice the squash in half lengthwise and place in roasting pan. Brush olive oil over the squash and sprinkle with dried thyme. Roast in a 400° oven for 1 hour. Remove from oven, cool, and then puree in food processor. Set aside. (May be prepared ahead.)

Melt 6 tablespoons of butter in large skillet. Add the green onions, garlic and chilies. Sauté lightly and add the squash. Stir for 2 minutes and add the fresh thyme, tarragon and parsley. Season with salt and pepper and cook, covered, for 3 minutes.

Heat the chicken stock in a large stock pot and add the squash mixture. Cook, covered over low heat for 5 minutes. Set aside. Meanwhile, remove meat from the two chicken breasts and chop into small pieces. (Save the rest of the boned chicken for laster use.) In a skillet over a medium-high heat, melt 6 tablespoons butter. Sauté the chicken until golden and slightly crispy.

Add the chicken and mushrooms to the hot stock. Correct the seasonings and stir in the sour cream. Serve piping hot with a fresh baguette, garnishing each bowl with fresh chopped parsley.

Health conscious people are eating more and more garlic. It is a staple in Spanish cuisine.

"Churros" are delicious fried dough sticks sprinkled with sugar and enjoyed with coffee or hot cocoa.

Ensalada de los Moros
(Moorish Salad)

1 cup extra virgin olive oil
4 tablespoons white wine vinegar
1 teaspoon paprika
2 heads bibb lettuce
3 tomatoes, cut in wedges
2 Spanish red onions, sliced thin into rings
3 hard-boiled eggs, chopped
48 black pitted olives
3/4 pounds fresh tuna steak, grilled or blackened

Season tuna steak with blackening spice or salt and pepper. Cook until done and cool. (May be prepared ahead.) Flake.

Mix oil, vinegar and paprika for vinaigrette. Place lettuce leaves on individual plates, arrange tomatoes, tuna (flaked), onion rings, olives and eggs over lettuce, and top with vinaigrette. Grind fresh pepper over each salad if desired.

Cocino Asado
(Roast Suckling Pig)

1 20-pound fresh "dressed" pig (or as available), head on,
   allowing one pound or more per person.
Salt and black pepper

Gravy
2 cups veal or beef stock
1/2 cup white Vermouth or white wine
1 teaspoon Dijon mustard
1 tablespoon flour

Order a young suckling pig from a butcher shop or farmer's market. The ideal size would be 20 pounds or smaller. (If you are only able to get a larger pig, cut it in half length-wise, freeze extra portion for later, cooking even the head separately, and re-assembling at "presentation" time before serving.)

Using the largest shallow roasting pan (a large jelly roll pan will do), line with heavy duty foil leaving 3 to 4 inches around each side. Place rack on pan. Preheat oven to 400°. Score the skin of the pig with a very sharp knife every 1-1/2 inches. Generously salt and pepper and place skin side up on the roasting pan. Use 2 pans and 2 ovens if necessary if pig is cut in half. Bake at 400° until skin begins to brown and sizzle, about 45 minutes. Reduce heat to 325° and continue cooking. Do not baste. To keep drippings from burning, add a small amount of water to the pan if necessary, being careful not to let the pig steam. Use a meat thermometer to tell when the meat is done. Total cooking time will be about 3 to 3-1/2 hours. Under broiler, crisp the skin until it bubbles, watching it very closely as it will burn easily. Remove pig from pan and allow to cool, uncovered for 20 minutes.

To prepare gravy, skim or pour off the fat from the baking pan, reserving all the pan juices and drippings. Add the veal or beef stock, or beef bouillon dissolved in 2 cups water, white vermouth or white wine, Dijon mustard and the flour paste for thickening. Bring to a boil, scraping pan well, and adding water as necessary. Pass at the table in a heated gravy boat.

If you have the head on the pig, put a flower in its mouth and present your crispy creation to your guests before carving. Be sure to give each person a piece of the crispy skin along with the meat and ribs.

In Spain, roast suckling pig is usually eaten without any sauce other than its own juices. However, we have served it with a simple gravy.

❦

¡Salud, amor y pesetes y el tiempo para gustarlo!

"Health, love and money and the time to enjoy them!"

Arroz Primavera con Azafran
(Saffron Rice with Spring Vegetables)

8 cups canned vegetable broth
2 cups chicken broth
2 pounds fresh asparagus, cut into 3 inch pieces
1-1/2 cups dry white wine
1 teaspoon saffron threads
1/2 cup (1 stick) butter
4 cups Arborio rice
2 teaspoons salt
2 red bell peppers, chopped
1 medium onion, chopped
1/2 cup grated Parmesan cheese

Bring broths to a boil in heavy large saucepan. Add asparagus pieces and cook 2 minutes. Remove asparagus and reserve. Add white wine and saffron threads to broth and simmer to keep hot. In a separate large saucepan, melt butter, sauté onions for 3 minutes until translucent, then add the chopped red pepper. Add rice and stir until rice is translucent for about 5 minutes. Reserving 1 cup broth/wine, add enough broth to cover rice completely. Stir continually, adding 1 cup broth at a time until all broth is absorbed. Simmer rice uncovered until tender and creamy, stirring occasionally. This will take about 30 minutes. (This may be done a little ahead, keeping the rice warm until ready to serve). Reheat if necessary and mix in asparagus, being careful not to break them. If the "arroz" seem too dry, add the remaining broth as needed. Sprinkle with Parmesan cheese when serving.

Saffron is costlier than gold. Fortunately, a little goes a long way! It is a key ingredient in the famous Spanish dish, "paella."

Tarta de los Musicianos
(Musician's Tart)

Crust
2 cups all purpose flour
1/2 teaspoon salt
1/4 cup sugar
3/4 cup unsalted butter (1-1/2 sticks)
3/4 teaspoon vanilla extract
1 large egg yolk
3 tablespoons whipping cream

Filling
1/2 cup pear nectar
1/3 cup dark brown sugar
1-1/2 cups dried pears or dried apples, coarsely chopped
1-1/2 cups pitted, chopped dates

Topping
1/2 cup (1 stick) unsalted butter
1/4 cup light corn syrup
1/2 cup dark brown sugar
3/4 cup pine nuts
3/4 cup cashew nuts, roasted
3/4 cup toasted whole almonds
2 tablespoons whipping cream

Using food processor, prepare crust by cutting butter into flour, salt and sugar until mixture resembles coarse corn meal or cut in manually. Add egg yolk and vanilla, mixing quickly. Add cream to processor bowl gradually until stiff dough forms. Remove from bowl and form into a ball. Wrap and refrigerate until chilled (or overnight). Roll out dough on floured board or pastry cloth to a 14 inch circle, to fit into a 10 inch tart pan or spring form pan, allowing about 1 to 2 inches on the sides. Freeze in the pan for 15 minutes, then weigh down crust with pie weights or dried beans in foil. Bake at 350° for about 10 minutes, remove foil and beans, and continue baking for 20 minutes longer or until golden brown.

Prepare fruit filling by bringing all ingredients to a boil in a heavy saucepan. Stir, reduce heat and simmer for one minute. Cool slightly and puree mixture. Cool completely.

For topping, cook butter, sugar and corn syrup until sugar dissolves using low heat stirring constantly. Increase heat and bring to a vigorous boil for one minute. Remove from heat and immediately add the pine nuts, cashews and almonds and cream. Stir.

Heat oven to 400°. To assemble tart, spread filling smoothly in crust. Spread nut topping over filling. Bake 20 minutes until bubbly. Cool 10 minutes on rack. Loosen tart sides but do not remove. Allow to cool completely. Serve at room temperature, cutting the tart into wedges.

This is a very rich dessert, both in ingredients and tradition! Freshly brewed coffee is the perfect accompaniment.

Musicians entertaining in the countryside were paid with dried fruits and nuts and so the name "Musicians Tart."

You may make pear nectar in a juicing machine. It is sometimes hard to find.

Café Español is a rich, dark roast coffee enjoyed with milk (Café con leche) in the morning, or black at the end of a meal.

NOTES:

PRELUDE TO THE OPERA

Antipasto

Crostini Alle Olive

Proscuitto E Melone

Mellanzane Alla Mozzarella

Pepperoni Alle Acciughe

"Zuppa" of Leek and Portabella Mushrooms

Insalata di Fagioli and Salsiccia

Tomato Pesto Linquine Topped with Fried Calamari

Tiramisu Soufflé

Figs with Almond Mascarpone Filling

Caffè Romano Caldo

SERVES 12

Celebrating the fine art of music through the art of cooking is a lyrical experience.

Opening night of The Atlanta Opera is always a gala affair.

Create the ambience of the evening with music from the famous "Three Tenors,"

Pavarotti, Domingo and Carreras.

For a show stopping table, cut old sheet music and use for placecards or placemats.

Continue the black and white theme by using a black top hat to hold

pink and white lilies, pink autumn joy, leaves of hosta and ornamental grasses.

Lay opera gloves and opera glasses nearby. Add a bit of authenticity to your dinner

with background music by Verdi. Be prepared to take a bow after a standing ovation

at the conclusion of this lovely evening.

Antipasto

Antipasto means "before the meal." This course is meant to prepare the stomach for the ones to follow by stimulating the gastric juices. Served in minimal amounts, hot ones are served before a light meal and cold ones before a large meal. The visual arrangement of antipasto dishes is important. A blend of colors and garnishes is all part of the stimulation. The next four recipes are antipasto dishes.

Crostini Alle Olive
(Fried Bread with Olives)

16 ounces fresh porcini mushrooms
1/2 cup extra virgin olive oil
2 garlic cloves, peeled and chopped
Salt and freshly ground pepper
12 slices firm coarse textured bread
1 cup black olives, pitted

Wash, trim and slice the mushrooms. Heat half the oil in skillet over high heat. Add garlic and mushrooms and stir fry for 5 minutes or until tender. Add seasoning.

Toast the bread slices in 350° oven until golden brown. Combine olives and remaining oil in a food processor until puréed. Spread on toast, cover with mushrooms and serve.

Olive Oil - Most Italian recipes have one ingredient in common that is indispensable: extra virgin olive oil. An old Italian saying is, "Wine lifts the spirits, oil lifts the taste." Oil has a dominant role in all Italian kitchens.

Purchasing olive oil can be tricky. It is graded according to the acidity it contains, which is perceived as sharpness at the back of the mouth. Extra virgin has 1 percent acidity, virgin has 3 percent. The only sure way to determine your preference is by sampling different oils.

Crostini is Italian for "little crusts," a great way to use yesterday's bread.

Proscuitto E Melone
(Ham and Melon)

1 large honeydew melon, peeled, seeded and cut into 2 inch wedges
Freshly ground pepper
12 slices proscuitto

Gently wrap each melon wedge with slice of proscuitto. Sprinkle with pepper. Chill and serve.

Mellanzane Alla Mozzarella
(Grilled Eggplant Topped with Tomato and Mozzarella)

12 slices eggplant, cut 3/8 inch thick
12 tomato slices
12 fresh basil leaves
12 thin slices fresh mozzarella cheese
1/2 cup extra virgin olive oil
Salt and freshly ground pepper

Lightly sprinkle eggplant slices with salt on both sides. Flatten them between two plates and top with a weight. Let eggplant drain for about 1 hour. Salt the tomato slices and let them drain for an hour.

Pat the eggplant slices dry. Brush with a little olive oil and cook them on a hot grill for a few minutes on each side until tender. Let cool. Top eggplant slices with a tomato slice, mozzarella slice and basil leaf. Drizzle with oil, season with salt and pepper and serve.

Proscuitto is a raw ham with a slightly sweet flavor, primarily from the Parma region of Italy. Proscuitto is made from pigs fed on acorns and is aged for nine months.

Fresh mozzarella is available at Italian markets.

Eggplants are either male or female; look at the blossom end: if it's indented, it's a female; if it's smooth, it's a male. Males have fewer seeds and are less bitter. To remove bitterness, slice and sprinkle with salt, let stand 30 minutes, rinse and pat dry.

Pepperoni Alle Acciughe
(Peppers with Anchovies)

1 can anchovy fillets preserved in salt
3 bell peppers, each a different color (red, yellow, green, purple, orange)
1 tablespoon finely chopped fresh oregano
1 garlic clove, very thinly sliced
1 tablespoon capers, drained and finely chopped
Salt
1/4 cup extra virgin olive oil

Wash 4 or 5 anchovy fillets several times to get rid of salt. Cut into small pieces. Wash, dry and halve the peppers, remove seeds and ribs. Bake in a preheated 400° oven for 20 minutes. Remove from oven and let cool. Cut into strips.

Sprinkle oregano, garlic, capers and anchovies over peppers. Season with salt to taste. Drizzle with oil. Let stand 2 hours to blend flavors.

"Zuppa" of Leek and Portabella Mushrooms

1 stick unsalted butter
8 leeks, white and pale green parts only, chopped (about 6 cups)
2 medium onions, chopped
16 ounces portabella mushrooms, chopped
1/4 cup all purpose flour
3 cups chicken stock or canned low-salt broth
1/2 cup dry sherry
4 cups light cream
1/2 teaspoon cayenne pepper
Salt and ground white pepper to taste

Melt butter in heavy pot. Add leeks and onion, sautéing until tender, about 10 minutes. Add mushrooms and sauté 5 minutes. Reduce to low heat. Add flour, cook until thick, stirring as necessary. Gradually stir in stock and half of the sherry. Bring to a boil, stirring. Reduce heat and simmer till thick, about 10 minutes. Add cream. Stir in cayenne and season with salt and white pepper to taste. Can be prepared ahead and refrigerated.

When ready to serve, bring to simmer. Stir in remaining sherry and ladle into cream soup bowls. Garnish with fresh Italian parsley, if desired.

Emperor Nero was said to have eaten leeks several days a month to clear his voice.

Look for small to medium-sized unblemished leeks and clean thoroughly. Leeks have a tendency to be rather sandy in their multi-layered leaves.

Cannellini beans can be purchased in Italian markets or you may substitute great Northern white beans.

Benedetto sia'l giorno, e'l mesa, e l'anno.

"Blessed be the day, the month, the year."

Insalata di Fagioli and Salsiccia
(Bean and Sausage Salad)

2 pounds hot Italian sausage, sliced in half lengthwise
1 cup dry white wine
2 tablespoons olive oil
2 medium onions, chopped
2 red bell peppers, chopped
3 tablespoons fresh thyme, chopped
2 16-ounce cans cannellini beans, drained and rinsed
Assorted greens, such as arugula, red leaf, boston

Brown sausages in heavy skillet, piercing each piece with fork. Pour off excess fat. Add 1/4 cup wine. Cover and simmer over low heat for 5 minutes. Uncover, increase heat to medium high and cook until sausages are brown, about 8 minutes. Remove from pan and crumble.

Pour off all but 2 tablespoons drippings. Add oil and heat over medium low heat. Add onion, pepper and thyme and sauté until brown and slightly soft, about 10 minutes. Add remaining wine and adjust heat to high. Reduce to half, cooking approximately 3 more minutes. Add beans and sausage, stir until heated through.

Divide greens among 12 plates. Top with sausage mixture and serve.

Tomato Pesto Linquine
Topped with Fried Calamari

Pesto
2 cups sun dried tomatoes packed in oil, drained
1 cup grated Romano and Parmesan cheese combined
3/4 cup chopped fresh basil or 3 tablespoons dried basil
1 cup pine nuts, toasted
6 cloves garlic, crushed
1-1/2 cups olive oil

Fried Calamari
2 pounds squid tubes, cut into rings about 1/4 to 1/2 inch thick
2 eggs, beaten
1 cup flour
1 cup Italian bread crumbs
1 cup cooking oil
Salt and pepper

Linguine
2 pounds linguine
1/2 pound pancetta (Italian bacon) browned and broken into bite size pieces
Freshly grated Parmesan cheese
Salt and freshly ground pepper

For pesto: Combine tomatoes, basil, cheese, pine nuts and garlic in food processor. With machine running, add oil gradually until smooth paste is formed. (Can be prepared 2 weeks ahead of time and frozen, or covered and refrigerated. Bring to room temperature before using.)

For fried calamari: Combine flour and bread crumbs. Season with salt and pepper. Dip squid, a few pieces at a time, in egg, then into crumb mixture. Deep fry in very hot oil until browned, approximately 2 minutes. Be sure oil is very hot so that frying time is minimal. Cooking calamari too long will toughen it. This must be done at the last minute to insure crispness.

For linguine: Cook linguine in large pot of salted boiling water, until tender but firm (al dente). Drain, reserving 1-1/2 cups of the liquid in the pot. Combine half the pesto with cooking liquid. Add linguine and toss to coat, adding pesto as desired. Season to taste.

Serve pasta topped with fried calamari, pass freshly grated Parmesan cheese.

Parmigiano-Reggiano is the best Parmesan you can purchase. It is produced in the countryside of Parma, Italy. It is expensive but worth every penny. It is easily recognized by its sweet, nutty flavor. The name should be stamped on the side of the rind.

Pancetta is a thick Italian bacon with a salty taste and is used to flavor recipes. It is not usually eaten alone.

Tiramisu Soufflé

2 envelopes unflavored gelatin softened in 1 cup cold water
1 cup water
1 cup sugar
4 eggs, separated
8 ounces cream cheese
3 tablespoons Tiramisu liqueur
3 tablespoons brandy
1/2 pint heavy cream, whipped
2 cups berries, in season
Shaved white or dark chocolate

Stir softened gelatin over low heat to dissolve. Add remaining water. Remove from heat and blend in 3/4 cup sugar. Beat egg yolks and add to mixture. Return to heat and cook 5 to 8 minutes, until thick. Add to softened cream cheese, mixing well until well blended. Stir in liqueur and brandy. Chill until slightly thick. Beat egg whites until soft peaks form. Gradually add remaining 1/4 cup sugar, beating until stiff. Fold in egg whites and whipped cream. Wrap a 3 inch collar of aluminum foil around top of 1-1/2 quart souffle dish. Secure with tape. Pour mixture into dish and chill until firm.

Spoon into stemmed sherbet dishes. Top with berries of your choice and shaved white or dark chocolate.

Figs with Almond Mascarpone Filling

16 ounces mascarpone cheese
6 tablespoons powdered sugar
4 tablespoons sour cream
24 fresh figs
1/2 cup chopped almonds
1 teaspoon ground cinnamon
4 tablespoons amaretto

Blend cheese, sugar and sour cream until smooth. Stir in chopped almonds. Slit each fig and squeeze gently to open. Spoon cheese mixture into each fig. Sprinkle with cinnamon and drizzle with Amaretto.

To serve: Assemble attractively on platter and pass.

Holiday

'TIS THE SEASON ...

Brie with Sun Dried Tomatoes

Shrimp and Saga on Crostini

Fresh Mushroom Vermouth Soup

Pomegranate and Spinach Salad
with Warm Champagne Dressing

Holiday Stuffed Beef Tenderloin

Duchess Potato Rings with Bronzed Carrots

Sautéed Snow Peas and Cherry Tomatoes

White Chocolate Mousse Cake with Cranberries Jubilee

SERVES 12

"Deck the halls with boughs of holly,
Fa la la la la, la la la la
Tis the season to be jolly!
Fa la la la la, la la la la"

Planning for a dinner party early in the season is sure
to put you in the holiday spirit.
The key to entertaining is early preparation…so,
force lots of narcissus and amaryllis bulbs at varying intervals
during November. Bring those beautiful old linens
out of the closet that you have been saving and use them!
Mix and match monogrammed damask napkins with lace-edged linen ones
and tuck them inside a variety of collected napkin rings.
Arrange a single amaryllis among blooming narcissuses
and variegated trailing ivy in a
large ceramic container (majolica or similar).
According to the size of your container, you may add
varieties of begonias or other attractive plants
that will enhance your color scheme.
Cover the entire base of plants with a velvety moss.
This arrangement (refreshed with new blooms
of amaryllis and narcissus)
will last the entire holiday season,
so relax and enjoy!

Brie with Sun Dried Tomatoes

1 15-ounce round of Brie
2 tablespoons minced parsley leaves
2 tablespoons freshly grated Parmesan cheese
1/2 cup sun dried tomatoes in oil, drained and minced
1 tablespoon oil from sun dried tomatoes
2 to 3 cloves garlic, minced
2 tablespoons fresh basil, minced
3 tablespoons pine nuts, toasted, salted and coarsely chopped
Crackers to serve

Chill Brie well before removing rind from the top. Place cheese on the serving platter. Combine parsley, Parmesan, tomatoes, oil, garlic, basil, and pine nuts. Spread on top of the cheese. Refrigerate.

To serve: Let Brie stand at room temperature for 30 to 60 minutes. Serve as a spread with crackers.

Shrimp and Saga on Crostini

24 uncooked large shrimp
1 tablespoon Celebration Seasoning *
3 tablespoons unsalted butter, melted
3 tablespoons olive oil
24 1/3-inch-thick French bread baguette slices
6 ounces saga cheese (or bleu cheese), room temperature
6 sprigs fresh rosemary, stems removed, leaves chopped

Cook shrimp in boiling water with Celebration Seasoning until just pink (about 2 minutes). Drain and cool. Peel and devein shrimp. Combine butter and oil and brush on one side of baguette slices. Broil until light brown on both sides. Cool to room temperature.

Spread cheese on buttered side of baguette slices. Top each with a shrimp. Broil until cheese melts and shrimp are heated through (about 2 minutes). Sprinkle with rosemary and serve.

* See recipe for Celebration Seasoning, page 14, side note.

Collect vintage silverplate baroque forks. They can be dipped in a gold wash for a wonderful and expensive look.

"A feast is made for laughter, and wine maketh merry."

Ecclesiastes 10:19

Fresh Mushroom Vermouth Soup

20 ounces mushrooms, finely chopped
12 ounces mushrooms, sliced
3/4 cup butter
3 cups finely chopped onion
1 teaspoon sugar
1/3 cup flour
2 cups water
3 1/2 cups chicken broth
2 cups dry vermouth
1 tablespoon salt
1/2 teaspoon pepper
Parsley sprigs

Sauté onions and sugar in the butter until golden. Add sliced and chopped mushrooms and sauté 5 minutes. Stir in flour until smooth and cook 2 minutes stirring constantly. Add water and stir until smooth. Add remaining ingredients and heat to boiling, stirring constantly. Reduce heat and simmer uncovered for 10 minutes. Can be refrigerated at this point.

To serve: Reheat and simmer for 10 minutes. Check seasonings and serve very hot, garnishing each bowl with a sprig of parsley.

Pomegranate and Spinach Salad with Warm Champagne Dressing

—••●••—

3 bunches spinach torn into bite size pieces
2 medium-size avocados, pitted, peeled, and thinly sliced
Seeds of two pomegranates (about 1 cup)

Warm Champagne Dressing
1/2 cup Champagne vinegar
1 tablespoon sugar
1 tablespoon all-purpose flour
1-1/2 teaspoons dry vermouth
1/2 teaspoon Dijon mustard
1 small egg, beaten
2 tablespoons heavy cream
1 cup olive oil
Salt and freshly ground black pepper, to taste

    Combine the vinegar, sugar, flour, vermouth, and mustard in a small saucepan. Heat to simmering over medium heat. Gradually whisk in the egg and cream over low heat. Whisk in the oil in a thin steady stream. Season with salt and pepper to taste. Remove from the heat.
    To serve: Place spinach leaves on each salad plate, fan the avocado slices in a circle around the edge of the greens with the pomegranate seeds in the middle. Pour a little dressing over each salad.

To speed up the ripening of an avocado, wrap it in a newspaper and place it in a brown paper bag. Leave it at room temperature for several hours or overnight.

With the children, sprout a plant by suspending the avocado pit over a glass of water with 3 toothpicks broad side of pit down.

Caution: "seeding" a pomegranate can blacken your fingers and nails. Use gloves or do ahead.

Holiday Stuffed Beef Tenderloin

•◦●●◦•

Beef

Two 2-3/4 to 3-pound beef tenderloins, trimmed of outside
    fat and double butterflied
Olive oil
1 tablespoon fresh rosemary, chopped or 1/2 teaspoon dried
1/4 cup olive oil
4 garlic cloves, flattened
8 bacon slices, halved crosswise
Salt and freshly ground pepper

Filling

7 to 8 tablespoons olive oil
5 large onions, thinly sliced
4 large red bell peppers, thinly sliced
5 large garlic cloves, minced
1-1/2 tablespoons fresh rosemary, chopped or 1-1/2 teaspoon dried
24 ounces fresh shiitake mushrooms (or 6 ounces dried shiitake
    mushrooms soaked until softened), thinly sliced, stems discarded
1 cup minced fresh parsley
Salt and freshly ground pepper

Sauce

Pan drippings from roasting pan used to cook beef
3 cups unsalted beef stock
4 tablespoons brandy
2 tablespoons Dijon mustard
1-1/2 teaspoons fresh rosemary, chopped or 1/2 teaspoon dried
6 tablespoons (3/4 stick) butter
Salt and freshly ground pepper
4 tablespoons minced fresh parsley
Fresh parsley sprigs for garnish

To prepare beef: Double-butterfly each tenderloin: the first slit is made 1/3 down from top on right side of meat, a lengthwise cut is made 3/4 of the way though the meat. The double butterfly is completed by a second slit made 1/3 up from the bottom of tenderloin on the left, cut 3/4 of the way through. You may ask the butcher to do this process. Place a plastic bag on work surface. Open tenderloins on bag and top with another plastic bag. Pound to flatten to 1/2 inch thickness. Arrange meat on work surface, cut side up. Rub with oil, rosemary, salt and pepper.

For filling: Heat 5 tablespoons oil over medium heat. Add onions and cook until translucent. Add bell peppers and cook for 3 minutes. Add 2 tablespoons oil, garlic and rosemary, mushrooms, salt and pepper, sauté for 3 minutes or until vegetables are just tender. Cool completely, add fresh parsley.

Mound 2 cups of filling down full length of each tenderloin (running in the same direction as cuts). Bring meat up around filling. Tie string around ends of each tenderloin, then around length. Tie crosswise at 1 inch intervals, pushing in filling. Reserve remaining filling for garnish. (Can be prepared up to 6 hours ahead. Rub outside of meat with olive oil. Refrigerate meat and remaining filling separately.

To cook: Preheat oven to 375°. Heat 3 to 4 tablespoons oil and garlic in heavy large skillet over medium-high heat. Cook until garlic is golden brown on both sides, about 2 minutes. Discard garlic. Pat meat dry; season with salt and pepper. Brown lightly, about 1 minute per side. Arrange in roasting pan, seam side down. Pour off all but film of fat from skillet and reserve skillet for mustard sauce preparation. Drape bacon over meat. Roast until thermometer inserted horizontally through end of roast into meat registers 125 to 130° for rare, about 30 minutes. Transfer roast to platter and tent with foil to keep warm: reserve drippings in roasting pan.   For sauce: In reserved skillet, add drippings from roasting pan. Add 1-1/2 cups stock scraping up any browned bits. Boil until reduced to thick syrup (about 1/2 of mixture), about 4 to 5 minutes. Add any drippings accumulated on meat platter, brandy, mustard, rosemary, and remaining 1-1/2 cups stock and boil until thickened, about 3 minutes. Reduce heat to medium and whisk in butter 1 tablespoon at a time. Add parsley and season with salt and pepper.

To serve: Rewarm reserved filling from refrigerator in skillet over medium-high heat. Remove bacon and string from roast. Cut roast across grain into 1/2-inch thick slices. Arrange 2 slices on each heated plate. Spoon sauce over slices. Place heated filling alongside. Garnish with fresh parsley sprigs.

For dried shiitake mushrooms, soak in hot water to cover until softened, 30 minutes. Drain. Squeeze out excess moisture and slice, discarding hard stems.

❦

A fine cut of beef is still a treat, even though people seem to be eating less red meat.

Duchess Potato Rings with Bronzed Carrots

Potato Rings
1 cup coarsely grated sharp cheddar cheese
6 cups mashed potatoes seasoned with salt and pepper, cooled
2 tablespoons (1/4 stick) melted butter

Bronzed Carrots
2 to 3 pounds carrots (tiny French or Belgian variety preferred),
    peeled and julienned (leave whole if small)
4 tablespoons butter
2 teaspoons sugar
Salt and freshly ground pepper
2 tablespoons brandy
Parsley sprigs for garnish

Potato Rings: Fold the cheese into the mashed potatoes. Shape the potato mixture into 12 individual rings and place on a cookie sheet. Brush with 1 tablespoon of butter. Bake at 350° until heated. Brush potato rings with remaining butter and broil 3 to 5 minutes until crisp and browned.

Bronzed Carrots: Combine carrots, butter and sugar in saucepan. Add just enough water to cover bottom of pan. Place over medium heat, cover and simmer until tender, checking occasionally and adding more water as necessary. Increase heat to high, add brandy, remove cover and boil until all liquid has evaporated. Season with salt and pepper to taste. Fill center of potato rings with carrots. Garnish with parsley.

Sautéed Snow Peas and Cherry Tomatoes

2 tablespoons olive oil
2 large garlic cloves, minced
24 small cherry tomatoes, stemmed
1 pound snow peas
1/2 cup pine nuts, toasted
1/4 cup chopped fresh basil or 1 tablespoon dried basil
3 tablespoons red wine vinegar
Salt and pepper to taste
Fresh basil leaves for garnish

Sauté garlic, tomatoes, and snow peas in oil (about 5 minutes). Add pine nuts, basil, and vinegar and stir 1 minute. Season with salt and pepper. Garnish with fresh basil leaves and serve.

White Chocolate Mousse
Cake with Cranberries Jubilee

━◦●●◦━

Crust
1-1/2 cups vanilla wafer cookie crumbs (about 4 to 5 ounces)
4 tablespoons unsalted butter, melted

Chocolate Mixture
9 ounces white chocolate, chopped
1 cup sugar
1/3 cup water
6 large egg whites
Pinch of cream of tartar

Cream Mixture
2 cups chilled whipping cream
1-1/2 tablespoon Grand Marnier or other orange liqueur
1-1/2 teaspoons vanilla
3 ounces white chocolate, chopped
1/4 cup chopped pistachios

Cranberry Jubilee Sauce
2 cups fresh cranberries or frozen unsweetened, thawed
1 cup water
1 cup sugar
1/8 teaspoon cinnamon
3 tablespoons rum

For crust: Mix together crumbs and butter and press into bottom of a 10-inch spring form pan. Refrigerate.

Chocolate mixture: Melt 9 ounces white chocolate in top of double boiler set over simmering water, stirring until smooth. Cool slightly until warm. Bring sugar and water to a boil in saucepan, stirring until sugar dissolves. Continue boiling and stirring until candy thermometer registers 238° (soft-ball stage). In a bowl, beat egg whites with cream of tartar until soft peaks form. Gradually beat hot sugar syrup into egg whites. Continue beating until mixture is stiff and glossy and bottom of bowl cools to barely lukewarm, about 3 minutes. Fold warm chocolate mixture into egg white mixture.. Refrigerate until cool but not set, about 5 minutes.

Cream mixture: Whip together cream, Grand Marnier, and vanilla until soft peaks form.

To assemble: Gently fold cream mixture into chocolate mixture. Fold in chopped white chocolate. Pour into crust; smooth top with spatula. Sprinkle top with chopped pistachios. Cover with plastic wrap and freeze until firm, about 6 hours.

"The only gift is a portion of thyself...."

Ralph Waldo Emerson

❧

Cranberry "bogs" are common in the wetlands of New England.

❧

Native American Indians used cranberries for war paint and dye, as well as a food staple.

Cranberry Jubilee Sauce: Combine sugar, water and cinnamon. Boil 5 minutes. Add cranberries and boil an additional 5 minutes. Heat rum and flame. Pour over cranberries.

To serve: Remove mousse from freezer and release pan sides. Cut dessert into wedges. Top with warm Cranberry Jubilee Sauce.

* Mousse Cake can be prepared 3 days ahead.

CHAMPAGNE AND CAVIAR CHRISTMAS

Elegant Caviar Tarte

Champagne Oysters and Shrimp

Roasted Chestnut Bisque

Chilled Romaine with Hot Brie Dressing

Fruit-Filled Christmas Goose

Wild Rice with Sausage and Prunes

Green Bean Bundles

Cappucino Fantasy

SERVES 12

The sparkle of champagne exudes romance and celebration.
Continue this feeling by playing
your favorite piano Christmas classics in the background.
Welcome your guests by illuminating your walkways,
adding a glorious holiday wreath on your front door
and festooning the house with holiday greens.

For this festive evening, set your table with lots of sparkle
by using silver chargers under your best formal china.
Use a low silver container filed with spruce, pine,
white roses, white lilies and variegated ivy.
Add silver Christmas ornaments
to the arrangement for even more sparkle.
Cluster a mixture of silver and crystal candlesticks
using especially long candles for a flamboyant effect.
Tie napkins with silver ribbons
or use antique silver napkin rings.
Miniature silver picture frames with guests names inscribed inside
can be used as placecards and given as individual gifts
for the guests to take home.

After dinner, entertainment can take different forms.
We like to ask a guest to bring a guitar
or gather around a piano to sing our favorite Christmas carols.

Elegant Caviar Tarte

6 hard-boiled eggs, peeled and finely chopped
1/4 cup butter, softened
2 teaspoons chopped fresh dill
1 teaspoon Dijon mustard
1 teaspoon red wine vinegar
1/8 teaspoon salt
6 green onions, white and green parts, finely chopped
1 8-ounce package cream cheese, softened
1/2 cup sour cream
1 to 2 tablespoons mayonnaise
1 small (2-ounce) jar red lumpfish caviar
1 small (2-ounce) jar black lumpfish caviar
Lemon slices and dill sprigs for garnish

Mash eggs and combine with butter, dill, mustard, red vinegar and salt. Spread mixture into a 9 inch pie plate. Sprinkle green onions over egg mixture. Blend together cream cheese and sour cream and spread over the green onions. Cover the pie plate with plastic wrap. Refrigerate until firm, 2 to 4 hours.

Spread a thin layer of mayonnaise over the cream cheese mixture. Decorate the top with a design of choice, using spoonfuls of both caviars. Garnish. Serve with gourmet crackers or plain bagel chips.

Centerpieces can be conversation pieces and contribute to the atmosphere but they should never dominate the table. Guests should always be able to see over the tablepiece. Almost anything can be used effectively as a centerpiece.

Use your imagination!

Champagne Oysters and Shrimp

36 fresh large oysters, shucked, reserving liquid
1/2 pound medium sized shrimp, shelled, deveined and coarsely chopped
6 tablespoons butter
1/2 cup milk
3 to 4 tablespoons champagne (or dry white wine)
3 tablespoons all purpose flour
1 egg yolk
1/4 teaspoon freshly ground white pepper
1 teaspoon salt
3/4 cup fresh bread crumbs
1 cup freshly grated Gruyère or Emmentaler cheese

Preheat oven to 450°. Melt 2 tablespoons butter in small skillet. Drop in the shrimp and cook over moderate heat, stirring constantly for 2 to 3 minutes, until they begin to turn pink. Set aside.

Measure the oyster liquid and add enough milk to make 1-3/4 cups. Stir in the champagne. In a heavy 8 or 10 inch skillet, melt the remaining 4 tablespoons of butter over moderate heat, but do not let it brown. Then stir in the flour and mix thoroughly. Pour in the oyster liquor mixture and stirring constantly with a whisk, cook over high heat until the sauce boils and thickens slightly. Reduce the heat to low and simmer for about 3 minutes. Then beat the egg yolk lightly in a bowl. Add about 1/4 cup of the sauce and whisk the egg yolk mixture into the sauce in the pan. Season with white pepper and salt. Remove the skillet from the heat and stir in the reserved shrimp.

Spoon about 1 tablespoon of the shrimp sauce into a ramekin. Top with 3 oysters and blanket the oysters with a second spoonful of the shrimp sauce. Place the filled ramekins on cookie sheets and bake in the top third of the oven for about 10 to 12 minutes or until sauce begins to bubble. Sprinkle the oysters evenly with the bread crumbs and the cheese. Return them to the oven for another 4 to 5 minutes or until the cheese melts and the crumbs brown slightly. You may then slide the cookie sheet under the broiler, about 3 inches from the heat, for a couple of minutes to further brown the tops.

Serve at once.

Roasted Chestnut Bisque

1 pound raw chestnuts in shells
1/4 cup unsalted butter
1/4 cup chopped bacon, cooked and crumbled (2 to 3 slices)
1/4 cup chopped prosciutto
1 large yellow onion, chopped
4 ribs celery, chopped
2 carrots, peeled and chopped
1 tablespoon fresh thyme
1 tablespoon fresh chervil
Salt and freshly ground white pepper, to taste
1 cup dry white wine
6 cups chicken broth
3/4 cup raw hazelnuts (about 1/2 pound in shell), shelled
1 cup milk
1/2 cup whipping cream
1/4 cup brandy
Crème fraîche to garnish *

Preheat oven to 350°. With a sharp knife, cut an "X" on the flat side of each chestnut. Bake in a roasting pan until both the outer shell and inner skin can easily be removed, 20 to 30 minutes. Let the nuts cool slightly and then shell them. Do not turn off the oven.

Melt the butter in a large stock pot over medium heat. Add the bacon, prosciutto, onion, celery, carrots, thyme, chervil, and salt and pepper to taste. Sauté until the vegetables begin to soften, about 10 minutes. Add the wine and stock. Stir in the chestnuts. Heat to boiling. Reduce heat and simmer uncovered 45 minutes. While the soup is simmering, toast the hazelnuts in the oven until they begin to turn brown, 15 to 20 minutes.

Remove from the oven and rub the nuts back and forth in a kitchen towel to remove the skins. Let the nuts cool, then chop them coarsely by hand or in a food processor fitted with a steel blade and set aside. When the soup has simmered for 45 minutes, remove it from heat and stir in the milk, whipping cream and brandy.

Purée the soup in batches in a blender or food processor fitted with a steel blade, adding a handful of hazelnuts to each batch. Pour into a clean pot, taste and adjust seasonings, and gently heat the soup until hot. Ladle into soup cups and garnish each serving with a dollop of crème fraîche.

* Crème fraîche - see recipe on page 5.

Thin soups can be garnished with herb sprigs which float on the surface. Thick soups can be dotted with crème fraîche or yogurt. Use a knife to push the cream out toward the bowl rim at equal intervals to form a sunburst pattern.

An easy way to puree soups is by using a hand-held portable blender directly in the soup pot. This greatly simplifies clean-up.

Chilled Romaine with Hot Brie Dressing

2 large head Romaine lettuce, torn in bite-sized pieces and chilled
Homemade garlic croûtons

Dressing
1/2 cup olive oil
4 teaspoons minced shallots
2 teaspoons minced garlic
1/2 cup sherry wine vinegar
2 tablespoons fresh lemon juice
4 teaspoons Dijon mustard
10 ounces ripe French Brie cheese (rind remains), cut into small pieces, room temperature
Freshly ground pepper

Croûtons
3 cups French bread cubes
1/4 cup olive oil
1 clove garlic, minced

To make croûtons, sauté garlic in oil in large skillet. Add cubes of French bread and stir until lightly browned on all sides.

Warm olive oil in heavy skillet over low heat for 10 minutes. Add shallots and garlic and cook until translucent, stirring occasionally, about 5 minutes. Blend in vinegar, lemon juice and mustard. Add cheese and stir until smooth. Season with pepper.

To serve: Arrange greens on plates, drizzle with dressing and top with garlic croûtons.

Fruit-Filled Christmas Goose

Goose
2 11-pound geese
1 orange, halved
Salt and pepper
2 large onions, quartered
2 large Granny Smith apples, quartered
1 pound pitted prunes, left whole
Cayenne pepper
Salt and pepper

Gravy
Pan drippings
1 cup red wine
1-1/2 cups water
2 15-ounce can chicken broth
4 tablespoons flour
Salt and pepper to taste

To prepare the goose: Remove fat from the cavity of goose. Rub entire goose including cavity with orange half. Fill the cavity and neck with a mixture of the onions/apples/prunes. Season with salt and peppers. Pierce goose skin (not meat) all over with fork.

Place goose, breast side up, on a rack set in roasting pan. Roast at 375° for 30 minutes. Pour off accumulated fat every 30 to 45 minutes. Roast at 325° until meat thermometer inserted in thickest part of thigh registers 180° (about 3-1/2 hours). Baste frequently. Cover with foil if sufficiently browned. Transfer goose to heated platter.

To make gravy: Skim off any fat from surface of pan juices. Place pan over high heat. Add 3/4 cup wine and boil until reduced to glaze consistency, scraping bottom of pan, about 5 minutes. Whisk remaining 1/4 cup wine and flour in a small bowl until smooth. Add water and broth with flour mixture to pan. Bring to a boil, stirring constantly. Reduce heat and simmer until gravy thickens, about 5 minutes. Season with salt and pepper. Strain into serving dish.

Before carving, present geese on large platters with the fruit filling attractively arranged.

To serve: Carve geese and serve with gravy.

Goose fat is a French favorite.

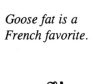

Reserve the goose fat that is rendered while roasting to use in cooking. It will keep in the refrigerator for one month.

"Why is there nothing so irrevocable as cooking your goose?"

Wild Rice with Sausage and Prunes

2 cups wild rice
8 cups chicken broth
1 cup white rice
1/2 pound diced smoked sausage
2/3 cup chopped onions
2/3 cup chopped green onions, green and white parts
1 cup chopped celery
12 pitted prunes, chopped
3 large tart apples, diced

Cook and stir diced sausage in a deep saucepan. Add the onions and celery; sauté for 2 to 3 minutes. Stir in the prunes, and add the apples. Cook for about 2 minutes. Remove from heat. Put wild rice in 8 cups of seasoned broth. Bring to a boil, stir and simmer for 30 minutes. Add 1 cup white rice to the wild rice and cook an additional 20 minutes, covered, until cooked and all liquid is absorbed. Combine with the sausage/apple mixture and serve hot.

Green Bean Bundles

3 pounds fresh green beans, cooked *al dente*
6 slices bacon, sliced in half
Pimento strips

Marinade
1/4 cup sugar
1 teaspoon celery seed
1 teaspoon dry mustard
1 teaspoon paprika
1 teaspoon salt
1 teaspoon minced onion
1 cup salad oil
4 tablespoons wine vinegar
2 cloves garlic

Drain beans. Using 5 or 6 beans per bundle, wrap bacon around them. Cut pimento into thin strips and wrap around bacon strips on beans. Combine all marinade ingredients in blender and pour over the beans. Marinate for 2 hours at room temperature. Remove bundles from marinade and place on rack on a broiler pan. Place in a preheated 300° oven for 30 to 40 minutes, or until bacon is cooked through. Serve hot.

Cappucino Fantasy

Crust
1/2 cup graham cracker crumbs
1/2 cup finely chopped walnuts
1 cup finely chopped almonds
1/4 cup sugar
6 tablespoons unsalted butter, melted

Chocolate Layer
2 cups heavy cream
16 ounces semisweet chocolate chips
2 tablespoons light corn syrup
1/2 cup (1 stick) unsalted butter, cut into pieces

Mocha Cream Filling
1 envelope unflavored gelatin
1 cup light cream
1/4 cup Kahlúa
1/4 cup semisweet chocolate chips
1/3 cup brown sugar
3 teaspoons instant coffee granules
2 egg yolks, beaten
2-1/2 cup whipping cream
2 tablespoons powdered sugar
1 tablespoon Kahlúa

Crust: Preheat oven to 350° and lightly oil a 9-1/2 x 2 inch springform pan.

In a bowl, stir together crust ingredients until combined well and press onto bottom of pan. Bake crust in middle of oven 15 minutes or until pale golden, and cool in pan on a rack.

Chocolate Layer: In a saucepan, heat cream, chocolate chips and corn syrup over moderately high heat, stirring occasionally, until chocolate is melted and mixture just comes to a boil. Remove pan from heat and stir in butter, one piece at a time, until smooth. Pour mixture over crust in pan and chill until firm, about 3 hours.

For Mocha Cream: Sprinkle gelatin over 1/2 cup cream in small saucepan. Let stand 1 minute. Add remaining light cream, sugar, chocolate chips, Kahlúa and coffee. Cook over low heat until granules dissolve and chocolate melts, about 2 minutes. Stir 1/4 mixture into egg yolks, stirring constantly, and add back to remaining hot mixture. Cook about 2 more minutes but do not boil. Remove from heat and cool till consistency of unbeaten egg white. Whip cream, gradually adding powdered sugar, and fold 2 cups into mocha cream mixture. Spread over chocolate layer. Cover and refrigerate until firm, about 4 hours.

Remove sides of springform pan. To remaining whipped cream, add 1 tablespoon Kahlúa. Frost sides and top edge with whipped cream and decorate with chocolate coffee beans.

We always end our holiday gourmet dinner with "The Twelve Days of Christmas" acting out with motions as we sing!

Chocolate coffee beans are available at specialty coffee shops.

NOTES:

SLEIGH BELLS AND STRUDEL

Prosciutto Wrapped Asparagus

Duck Breasts with Brandied Cherry Sauce

Sherried Pistachio Soup

Festive Greens with Cranberry Vinaigrette

Seafood Strudel

Lemon Rice Pilaf

Spinach Stuffed Plum Tomato

Gâteau Nègre Praliné

SERVES 12

This holiday menu includes some of our favorite things.

Share cherished memories with your guests.

Lop-eared teddy bears, alphabet blocks, toy soldiers or

the caboose of a childhood train set,

all add a charming touch to your sideboard or table.

Fragrant, native greenery of cedar, pine, holly and

juniper mix attractively with the berries of nandina and holly.

Be sure to include a few sprigs of wooly lambs ear

and aromatic rosemary to your arrangements.

Bottle green majolica dessert plates compliment our

traditional colors of red and green.

Add turned wooden candlesticks encircled with miniature ivy

to complete this nostalgic setting.

Prosciutto Wrapped Asparagus

• • • •

72 very thin asparagus spears
4 ounces fresh goat cheese at room temperature
    (such as Chèvre or Montrachet)
2 ounces cream cheese, softened
2 teaspoons grated orange peel
1/4 teaspoon lemon juice
3 tablespoons chopped fresh basil
2-1/2 tablespoons salted, toasted pine nuts, chopped
1-1/2 to 2 tablespoons water
5 ounces thinly sliced proscuitto, cut into 36 5-inch x 1-inch strips
Salt and pepper

    Cut stalks from asparagus, leaving 2-1/2 to 3 inch tips. Cook tips in boiling salted water for 1 minute or until crisp-tender. Drain well and transfer to paper towels.

    Mix cheeses, orange peel, lemon juice, basil, pine nuts and water in bowl. Season with salt and pepper. Spread thin layer of filling over each proscuitto strip. Place 2 asparagus tips on top of filling at one end of proscuitto. Roll up proscuitto, enclosing base of asparagus. Press to seal. Cover and chill before serving.

    Arrange in pinwheel fashion, garnishing with basil leaves and orange peel.

"The success of a dinner party can be judged by the manner in which conversation has been sustained."

American Etiquette 1882

If using larger asparagus, one will roll nicely.

Duck Breasts with Brandied Cherry Sauce

— • • • • —

Do not overcook duck breast or the tendons will become very tough. Duck lovers feel that it should be undercooked, and in fact, cooked for no longer than the time it would take to fly through the oven!

3 duck breasts, about 12 ounces each
Fresh thyme sprigs for garnish

Marinade
2 cloves garlic
2 sprigs fresh thyme
4 tablespoons brandy
Salt and freshly ground pepper

Sauce
1/2 cup chicken stock
Beurre Manié (2 tablespoons butter, 1 tablespoon flour)
Strained liquid from marinade
12 ounce package frozen dark cherries, halved

Wipe off the duck breasts (reserve marinade), prick the skin and in a greased heavy skillet over medium high heat, cook the duck breasts, skin side down, until brown. Turn and cook the other side until the duck is rare. Remove from skillet and keep warm. Pour off all the fat and deglaze the pan with chicken broth over low heat. Strain the marinade and add to the pan. Cook over medium heat until liquid is reduced by half. Whisk in the Beurre Manié and add the cherries, cooking for several minutes until very hot.

To serve: Thinly slice the duck and fan out 3 or 4 slices on each warm plate. Arrange the duck with the sauce and cherries, placing one or two cherry halves on top of each slices with a sprig of fresh thyme.

Sherried Pistachio Soup

— • • • • —

5 slices lean bacon, cut into pieces
1/2 cup finely chopped onion
1/2 cup finely chopped celery
2 cloves garlic, minced
1 bay leaf
1 teaspoon chervil leaves
2/3 cup dry Sherry
6 cups chicken stock
1/3 cup white rice
1-3/4 cups shelled, unsalted pistachio nuts
1/3 cup chopped fresh parsley
1-1/2 cups light cream
Salt and white pepper to taste

Sauté bacon until crisp. Remove and drain on paper towels. Pour off excess grease. Add celery, onion and garlic to pan and cook for 5 minutes. Combine bacon and vegetables in a large pot. Add bay leaf and sherry. Bring to a boil, reduce heat and cook until all wine evaporates. Stir in chicken stock and rice. Bring to a boil, reduce heat and simmer for 25 minutes or until rice is soft. Discard bay leaf.

Finely grind pistachio nuts in food processor. Remove 1/3 cup of the nuts and set aside. Puree the remaining nuts with broth, chervil leaves and parsley in batches until smooth. Return to pot and stir in cream. Season with salt and pepper. Serve hot. Garnish with reserved pistachio nuts.

Festive Greens with Cranberry Vinaigrette

2 cups tawny port wine
2/3 cup thinly sliced shallots
1-3/4 cups fresh cranberries
5 tablespoons raspberry vinegar
2/3 cup safflower oil
2 teaspoons natural sugar (or more to taste)
12 to 14 cups assorted greens (such as red leaf, romaine,
    Belgian endive) torn
1-1/2 cups crumbled Stilton cheese
1/2 cup chopped walnuts
Salt and pepper to taste

Boil port wine and shallots in heavy small sauce pan until liquid is reduced to 4 tablespoons, about 12 minutes. Add cranberries, oil, vinegar and sugar and boil 3 minutes. Let cool slightly and season with salt and pepper. Arrange greens on salad plates and drizzle vinaigrette over individual salads. Sprinkle with cheese and nuts. Serve warm.

Unsalted pistachios may be found at specialty markets.

Fine herbs, such as basil, chervil, tarragon and dill, have a more delicate flavor and should be added to dishes just before serving.

"Christmas has come; let every man eat, drink, be merry all he can; no matter what lies in the bowls, we'll make it rich with our souls."

William Henry Davies

Seafood Strudel

Cooking Tips: Dampen a dish towel, spread it on the counter, cover it with waxed paper. Unfold the phyllo sheets and put on the waxed paper. Fold the towel with the phyllo sheets in half like a book. Work from the front of the book to the middle and then from the back of the book to the middle and butter each sheet as if you were turning pages in a book. With the book opened spread all fillings on the lower third of the book so the strudel can be easily rolled after you have tucked in the left and right edges of the opened book.

Pastry
1 pound phyllo pastry sheets (1/2 pound per strudel, thawed)
1-3/4 cups (3-1/2 sticks) unsalted butter, melted

Seafood filling
3 pounds cleaned shelled cooked crab, partially cooked shrimp, lobster
    or halibut or combination, in bite size chunks

Sauce Filling
1/4 cup (1/2 stick) unsalted butter
1/4 cup all purpose flour
1 teaspoon Dijon mustard
1 teaspoon salt
1/2 teaspoon cayenne pepper
1-1/2 cups milk, room temperature
1/4 cup whipping cream

Breadcrumb Mixture
1-1/2 cups breadcrumbs
1/2 cup freshly grated Parmesan cheese
1/2 teaspoon dry mustard

Other filling ingredients
1-1/2 cups sour cream
1 cup grated Swiss cheese
4 hard cooked eggs, chopped
1/2 cup chopped parsley
1/2 cup diced shallots
1/4 cup chopped scallions
2 large garlic cloves, minced

For brushing
1/4 cup (1/2 stick) unsalted butter, melted

Garnish
1/4 cup freshly grated Parmesan cheese
1/2 cup minced parsley
Crab or lobster claws (optional)

For sauce: Melt butter in saucepan over low heat. Stir in flour and make a smooth paste, stirring constantly until mixture just begins to bubble, add mustard and seasonings. Slowly stir in milk over medium heat and cook, stirring constantly, until mixture bubbles and thickens. Add cream and additional seasonings to taste. Cover and chill until thick (about 2 hours).

Pastry Sheets: Divide phyllo into 2 equal stacks, one for each strudel. Butter each sheet according to directions on phyllo package and see cooking tips in side note on previous page. Phyllo thaws in package at room temperature for about 5 hours.)

Layer seafood on each 1/2 pound stack of buttered pastry sheets. Dot the seafood with sour cream. Combine bread crumbs, Parmesan, and dry mustard in a small bowl. Over seafood, sprinkle the bread crumb mixture, Swiss cheese, parsley, shallots, chives, and garlic. Lastly, spoon the chilled sauce over the seafood. Tuck in the ends by folding in (2-3 inches) the left and right edges of the pastry stack. Then roll the strudel in a jellyroll fashion into a long roll. Place the strudels seam side down on buttered baking sheets and brush the strudels with melted butter. (The strudels may be refrigerated or frozen here, covered after chilling a little while to harden the butter. If refrigerated, bring to room temperature before baking. If frozen, defrost for 30 minutes and increase baking time slightly.) Preheat oven to 375 and bake 12 minutes. Remove from oven, brush with butter and slice diagonally with a serrated knife into 1-1/2 inch pieces. Push slices back together to reshape loaf. Brush again. Repeat brushing 2 more times during baking an additional 35 to 40 minutes or until crisp and golden brown. Remove strudels from oven, brush with remaining butter, and let them sit for 10 minutes.

To serve: Place a slice on each plate and sprinkle with Parmesan and minced parsley and if desired, garnish with crab or lobster claws.

Makes 2 strudel seafood rolls.

It takes time to prepare this wonderful strudel, but it will be worth every minute!

Spinach Stuffed Plum Tomato

——————•◦●◦•——————

6 large plum tomatoes, halved lengthwise, pulp removed and discarded
2 bunches spinach leaves, cooked and drained
1 3 ounce package cream cheese
1 clove garlic, minced
1/2 teaspoon salt
1 teaspoon ground mustard
1 teaspoon sugar

Melt cream cheese and blend this together with all remaining ingredients. Spoon mixture into each tomato half. Can be refrigerated at this point.

To serve: Bake tomato halves at 350° until bubbly and then broil until lightly brown.

Lemon Rice Pilaf

6 tablespoons butter
4-1/2 cups long grain white rice
9 cups chicken stock
Salt to taste

Creamy Lemon Sauce
3 tablespoons fresh lemon juice
3 teaspoons grated lemon peel
6 yolks from extra large eggs
3/4 cup light cream

1/2 cup freshly grated Parmesan cheese
1/2 cup chopped fresh parsley leaves
Fresh ground pepper

Sauté rice for 1 to 2 minutes in the butter. Add chicken stock and salt. Cover and cook for 20 minutes, or until rice is tender and the liquid has been absorbed.

For Sauce: Combine lemon juice, lemon peel, yolks, and cream in a small bowl. Whisk them until well blended. Toss together rice, sauce, Parmesan cheese and parsley. Put mixture in a microwave dish, which may be refrigerated at this point.

Heat pilaf, covered, in microwave for approximately 5 minutes before serving.

Gâteau Nègre Praliné

Cake

1 cup unsalted butter at room temperature
1 cup plus 3 tablespoons superfine granulated sugar
5 large eggs at room temperature, separated
1 teaspoon almond extract
1/2 cup (scant) fine quality cocoa, sifted
1/2 cup ground pecans (pecan meal)
1/2 teaspoon cream of tartar *

Praline Sauce

3/4 cup brown sugar
3/4 cup white sugar
2 teaspoons white corn syrup
Dash salt
3 tablespoons evaporated milk
1 tablespoon butter
1 teaspoon vanilla extract
1 cup chopped pecans

Chocolate Whipped Cream

2 cups whipping cream
3 tablespoons cocoa, sifted
1/2 cup powdered sugar

For Cake: Preheat oven to 325°. Line two 9-inch round cake pans with waxed or parchment paper. Grease lightly. Cream butter, gradually add sugar and beat constantly. Add egg yolks and extract and beat until light and fluffy. Stir in cocoa and pecans until well blended. Beat egg whites with cream of tartar until stiff but not dry. Gently stir in 1/4 of the egg whites. When mixed, carefully fold in the remaining egg whites. Spoon into pans. Bake for 30 minutes. Let cake cool for several minutes, carefully invert onto a lightly buttered rack and remove the paper immediately.

For Praline Sauce: Combine the sugars, syrup, salt and milk in heavy saucepan. Bring to a boil and cook until sugars are dissolved. Remove from heat and add butter, vanilla and pecans. Stir well. Cool.

For Chocolate Whipped Cream: Sift cocoa and powdered sugar over 2 cups whipping cream in a chilled bowl. Whip to soft peaks.

To assemble cake: Place 1 layer on cake plate. Spread thin layer of chocolate whipped cream and about 3/4 cup of the praline sauce. Top with the second cake layer and repeat. Top with mounds of the whipped cream or pipe from a pastry bag. Drizzle the remaining praline sauce over the cake. Refrigerate for several hours before serving.

* If using a copper bowl, it is not necessary to use cream of tartar.

Placing a cream dessert in the freezer for 20 minutes before serving will make cutting easier.

NOTES:

AN ATLANTA CHRISTMAS

Shrimp Stuffed New Potatoes

Nutcracker Fettucini

Orange Carrot Soup

Lobster and Asparagus Salad

Peppercorn Crusted Roast Pork with Brandy Sauce

Cranberry Chutney

Seasonal Sage Stuffing

Petite Choco-mint Soufflés with Crème de Menthe Sauce

SERVES 12

"The Nutcracker" at the Fox Theater, "A Christmas Carol" at The Alliance Theatre, Symphony Hall for a Christmas concert and a gourmet dinner with good friends — these are all the essence of "An Atlanta Christmas."

With the arrival of the Christmas season, bring a festive air
to your rooms with evergreen garlands entwined with gold ribbons
and tiny white lights. This is especially effective on a sun porch
and a great place to serve this menu. Fill the porch with
white poinsettias. For this Christmas table setting,
use the elegant with the rustic. A simple floor length cloth
of beige cotton and ecru brocade napkins tied with gold cording
set the theme. Use small terra cotta pots sprayed gold
to hold votive candles at each place setting. Arrange two topiaries,
tall enough to clear the eye level of your guests, in rusty finished tole planters.
Flowers and green inserted in an oasis atop a gold sprayed branch will create an
elegant centerpiece. On small scrolls tied with ribbon,
give each guest a toast to read during the dinner.
Make this Christmas a celebration of friendship.

At Christmas, we cherish our traditions started long ago.
Holding hands before the meal, our host blesses the food.
Following our Christmas dinners, we like to sing
"The Twelve Days of Christmas."
Some in our group enthusiastically act out the lines,
while others just like to sing.

Shrimp Stuffed New Potatoes

—·●●·—

18 unpeeled small round red potatoes (about 3/4 pound)
12 ounces small fresh peeled shrimp, cooked and drained
1/2 cup water
2 tablespoon mayonnaise
2 tablespoon softened cream cheese
1 tablespoon sour cream
2 cloves garlic, minced
2 tablespoons green onion, finely minced
1 teaspoon lemon juice
1 to 2 sprigs fresh dill, minced
Salt and white pepper to taste
Fresh dill for garnish

Place potatoes in a large casserole. Add 1/2 cup water. Cover with plastic wrap and microwave for about 15 minutes, or until tender. Cool. Cut each potato in half and scoop center out, leaving a 1/4 inch shell. Salt and pepper the shells. Brush with melted butter, and broil until lightly browned.

Put the shrimp, mayonnaise, cream cheese, sour cream and next 5 ingredients in food processor. Process until smooth. Spoon 1 teaspoon shrimp mixture into each potato shell. Chill until ready to serve Top with a sprig of dill. Makes 3 dozen appetizers.

We use the microwave oven as a time saver as often as possible. Of course, these potatoes can be boiled on top of the stove for 15 to 20 minutes.

This season, share the gift of hospitality in your home. Starting with your front door, create a wreath made with fresh greenery and miniature pineapples, the traditional symbols of hospitality. Add additional fruits, such as oranges, apples and pomegranates, using some whole and some sliced. Fill in gaps with a few holly berries and attach hanger. Continue the fruit theme, arrange a centerpiece interspersed with grapes, frosted with a sprinkle of powder. Add glossy leaves, holly and magnolia sprayed lightly with snow. Artichokes with a hint of gold lend the final touch.

Nutcracker Fettucini

1-1/2 pounds tomato fettuccine (spiral tomato pasta may be used)
Red food coloring, optional
1 pint light cream
1 egg yolk, lightly beaten
1-1/2 cups grated Asagio cheese
3 tablespoons butter
Salt and white pepper
Cayenne
1 tablespoon olive oil
1 pound snow peas (or sugar snap peas)
2 red bell peppers, sliced
1 cup chopped hazelnuts

Cook the pasta in a large pot of boiling, lightly salted water. You may add 5 to 6 drops red food coloring to the water to help retain the red color of the pasta. Drain.

In a skillet or sauté pan, heat the cream to a simmer. Stir a little into the egg yolk, stirring constantly. Then add the yolk to the cream. Do not boil or the egg will curdle. Over low heat, stir in the cheese and butter, and season with salt, pepper, and cayenne to taste.

Sauté the peas and pepper slices for 2 to 3 minutes in the olive oil in a large skillet.

Gently toss the cooked pasta with the sauce, coating the noodles. Arrange the peas and red pepper in an attractive manner over the pasta. Sprinkle with nuts.

Orange Carrot Soup

4 tablespoons butter
1 tablespoon fresh ginger root, minced
1 cup onions, chopped
Salt and white pepper
2 pounds carrots, peeled and sliced
6 cups chicken broth
2 cups orange juice
2 oranges, peeled and sliced
Chives, either minced or left in longer strips for garnish

Sauté ginger and onions in large saucepan until onions are tender. Add 3 cups broth, carrots, salt and pepper and simmer for 20 to 30 minutes, or until carrots are tender. Puree in food processor or with a hand-held blender. Return to saucepan, add remaining 3 cups broth and orange juice.

To serve: May be served warm or chilled. Float chives and a slice of orange on top as garnish. Soup may be prepared a day ahead.

The combination of red and green in this dish makes it a festive holiday first course.

Hazelnut is a round, reddish nut, the fruit of a bush that grows wild in Europe. The nuts of the cultivated hazelnut bush are called filberts.

To remove skins from roasted hazelnuts, rub the nuts back and forth in a kitchen towel.

Although this soup is delicious when served chilled, at holiday time we prefer it hot.

Most men prefer hot soups!

Lobster and Asparagus Salad

—●●●—

2 to 3 large frozen rock lobster tails (at least 1-1/2 pounds)
1/2 teaspoon sugar
1/2 teaspoon salt
2 pounds asparagus, washed, trimmed and peeled

Dressing
3 hard cooked eggs
4 tablespoons tarragon vinegar
4 teaspoons finely minced shallots
4 teaspoons finely minced fresh chives
4 teaspoons finely minced fresh parsley
1/2 teaspoon salt
1/2 teaspoon Worcestershire sauce
Freshly ground pepper to taste
1/4 cup peanut, hazelnut or walnut oil

2 heads Boston lettuce, washed, trimmed and finely shredded

Cook lobster in a large saucepan of boiling water until tender, about 10 minutes. Drain well, then immediately plunge into ice water to stop cooking process. Discard shell. Halve tail lengthwise, then cut each half into 1/4 inch slices. Transfer to medium bowl.

Combine sugar and salt with 2 quarts water in large saucepan and bring to boil over high heat. Add asparagus and cook until crisp-tender, about 4 minutes. Drain well, then immediately plunge into ice water to stop cooking process. Let cool, drain again. Cut asparagus into 1 inch lengths. Add to lobster. Cover and refrigerate.

For dressing: Coarsely chop one hard boiled egg and set aside. Mince remaining eggs in food processor. Add next 6 ingredients with pepper and mix until blended, about 50 seconds. With machine running, add oils in a slow, steady stream and mix until thick and creamy. Transfer to medium bowl. Fold in chopped egg. (If dressing is too thick, thin with oil or vinegar.)

To serve: Divide lettuce among salad plates. Lightly toss lobster and asparagus and mound over lettuce. Top each serving with 1 to 2 generous spoonfuls of dressing.

Asparagus may be steamed in microwave for 6 to 7 minutes, covered, with 2 tablespoons of water.

Oops, it's burning! How burnt is it? Quickly change pots. If it is just a little burned, try the old potato trick. Add a peeled, quartered potato and let it simmer.

"Friendship you know is the shadow of the evening which strengthens with the setting sun of life."

Hilda Moreau

The flavor is stronger in freshly purchased peppercorns.

Cognac is a spirit distilled from wine and used to add flavor and aroma to many sauces.

For the freshest pepper flavor, always purchase whole peppercorns (white, black or green) and grind them yourself.

"Here is a toast to the host,
Who carved the roast;
Here is a toast to the hostess,
May she never roast us!"

Peppercorn Crusted Roast Pork with Brandy Sauce

1/2 cup plus 2 tablespoons unsalted butter, room temperature
1 6 to 7 pound boneless pork loin roast
4 tablespoon all purpose flour
3 tablespoons Dijon mustard
1 teaspoon dry mustard
1-1/2 tablespoons cracked black peppercorns
1-1/2 tablespoons cracked dried green peppercorns
1-1/2 tablespoons cracked white peppercorns
1 tablespoon whole mustard seeds
1 tablespoon golden brown sugar
1 tablespoon dried thyme, crumbled

Brandy Sauce
2 cups apple cider
1/3 cup cognac
3 to 4 tablespoons all purpose flour
1-1/2 cups chicken stock or canned broth
1-1/2 tablespoons cider vinegar
1 tablespoon Dijon mustard
Salt and pepper to taste

Preheat oven to 475°. Position rack in lowest third of oven. Melt 2 tablespoons butter in heavy large skillet over medium high heat. Add roast and cook until brown, about 4 minutes per side. Remove from skillet. Cool 10 minutes. Transfer to roasting pan.

Combine remaining 1/2 cup butter with flour, mustards, peppercorns, mustard seeds, sugar and thyme in a bowl. Spread paste over top and sides of roasts. Roast 30 minutes. Reduce heat to 325°. Continue cooking about 1 hour 20 minutes for medium.

Transfer roast to cutting board and tent with foil. Transfer 2 tablespoons drippings in pan to a heavy small saucepan; reserve remaining drippings in pan, pouring off excess fat.

For sauce: heat roasting pan over medium low heat. Add cider and boil until liquid is reduced to 3/4 cup, scraping up any browned bits, about 8 minutes. Stir in cognac; boil 1 minute. Heat drippings in saucepan over medium high heat. Add flour and stir until golden brown, about 2 minutes. Whisk in cider mixture and stock. Simmer until thickened, stirring occasionally, about 2 minutes. Remove from heat. Mix in cider vinegar and mustard. Season with salt and pepper. Carve pork and serve with sauce.

Cranberry Chutney

2 pounds fresh cranberries
1 cup golden raisins
8 ounces dried apricots, cut into pieces
1-1/4 cup red wine
2 cups cranberry juice
1 orange, sliced thin and quartered
1 lemon, sliced thin, quartered
1 lime, sliced thin, quartered
1 teaspoon cinnamon
1/2 teaspoon ginger
2 cups sugar
1 cup chopped walnuts

Mix all ingredients except sugar and nuts in a large pot. Simmer until fruit is tender. Add sugar, mix well, and cook over low heat until sugar is dissolved. Stir in nuts and serve.

This will keep in the refrigerator for several months. It's a great accompaniment to pork and is excellent with turkey and lamb.

Here's a toast:

"Here's to our friendship; May it be reckoned, Long as a lifetime, Close as a second."

"At Christmas play and make good cheer, For Christmas comes but once a year."

Seasonal Sage Stuffing

Cornbread
1 cup self-rising corn meal
1/2 cup self-rising flour
1/4 teaspoon salt
3 tablespoons vegetable oil
1/2 cup low-fat buttermilk
1 egg, beaten

Biscuit
2 cups self-rising flour
1/4 cup vegetable oil
2/3 cup buttermilk

Stuffing
2 to 3 tablespoons fresh sage leaves, chopped or 1 tablespoon dried
3 cups pork broth, hot (chicken broth may be substituted)
1 large onion, diced
3/4 cup celery, diced
3 large eggs, slightly beaten
1 3-ounce can evaporated milk
Salt and black pepper to taste

For cornbread: Combine dry ingredients. Stir in buttermilk, oil, and egg. Mix well. Pour into a well greased 8 or 9 inch heavy skillet. Bake at 425° about 20 to 25 minutes, until well browned.   Remove from skillet immediately.

For biscuit: Combine all ingredients. Pour into a lightly greased 9 inch pan or onto a cookie sheet. Bake at 425° until done, about 15 to 18 minutes.

For stuffing: Crumble corn bread and biscuits into a large bowl. Sprinkle chopped sage over bread mixture. Pour hot broth over bread. Mash with a potato masher until mixed well. Stir in eggs and milk. Add in onions, celery, salt and pepper. Mix well. Spray an 9 x 13 inch baking dish with cooking spray. Pour stuffing into dish. Bake at 400° approximately 45 to 55 minutes until center feels firm. Cover with foil for first 20 minutes of baking time.

Any uncooked stuffing mixture may be stored in the refrigerator for 2 days or may be frozen for later use.

Petite Choco-mint Soufflés
with Crème de Menthe Sauce

—••••—

Soufflés
1/2 stick butter
1/2 cup flour
1-1/3 cups milk
1 cup semisweet chocolate pieces
2/3 cup water   *Sauce*
1 cup superfine sugar   6 to 8 crushed candy canes
1-1/2 teaspoons vanilla extract   1 cup whipping cream
6 egg yolks   1/4 cup water
8 egg whites   1 tablespoon white
1/3 teaspoon cream of tartar   Crème de Menthe
4 6-inch long candy canes, crushed   liqueur

Prepare 12 individual 1 to 1-1/4 cup soufflé dishes (freezer to oven to table type) by buttering and sprinkling with sugar. Set aside.

Soufflés: Melt butter over medium heat and whisk in flour. Continue cooking until mixture is bubbly. Gradually whisk in the milk, bring to a boil and allow to thicken. Remove from heat and whisk in the chocolate pieces until melted and smooth. Add water, half the sugar and vanilla. Allow to cool to room temperature.

When mixture has cooled, whisk in egg yolks, one at a time, until well blended. Set aside.

Beat egg whites with the cream of tartar in a large bowl until soft peaks form. Gradually add the remaining sugar, beating constantly, until the sugar is dissolved. (When rubbed between two fingers, no sugar granules can be felt.) Whites should be stiff and glossy but not dry.

Fold 1/4 of the egg whites into the chocolate mixture. When well mixed, add the mixture to the rest of the beaten egg whites and gently fold. Do not over mix. Divide the mixture evenly among the 12 soufflé dishes. Sprinkle the crushed candy canes over soufflés. Place on a pan and wrap well with foil. Freeze for up to three days.

To bake, preheat oven to 400°. Place the soufflés in oven on the pan or baking sheet and bake until puffed and fairly firm to the touch but soft in the center (about 40 minutes). If soufflés are not frozen, bake only 30 minutes).

For sauce: Combine whipping cream, crushed candy canes and water in saucepan. Stir over medium heat until candy melts. Add the chocolate and stir until melted and smooth. Remove from heat and add the white Crème de Menthe. Serve warm with the baked soufflés. (This may be done ahead of time and reheated before serving.)

To serve: Present the puffed soufflés to your guests immediately upon removing from the oven. "Plunge" a spoonful of the sauce in the middle of each soufflé.

Superfine sugar is a finer granulated sugar, available usually in a one pound box, and better for dissolving in meringues.

Cream of tartar is used to add volume to whipped egg whites. If a copper bowl is used to whip the egg whites, the cream of tartar is not needed.

A miniature candy cane may be placed in the center of each soufflé for garnish.

NOTES:

INDEX
(All Recipes Serve 12)

METRIC SYSTEM

COMPARISON TO METRIC MEASURE

When You Know	Symbol	Multiply By	To Find	Symbol
teaspoons	tsp. or t.	5.00	milliliters	ml
tablespoons	tbsp. or T.	15.00	milliliters	ml
fluid oz.	fl. oz.	30.00	milliliters	ml
cups	c.	0.24	liters	l
pints	pt.	0.47	liters	l
quarts	qt.	0.95	liters	l
ounces	oz.	28.00	grams	g
pounds	lb.	0.45	kilograms	kg
Fahrenheit	F	5/9 (after subtracting 32)	Celsius	C

LIQUID MEASURE TO LITERS

1/4 cup	=	0.06	liters
1/2 cup	=	0.12	liters
3/4 cup	=	0.18	liters
1 cup	=	0.24	liters
1-1/4 cups	=	0.3	liters
1-1/2 cups	=	0.36	liters
2 cups	=	0.48	liters
2-1/2 cups	=	0.6	liters
3 cups	=	0.72	liters
3-1/2 cups	=	0.84	liters

LIQUID MEASURE TO MILLILITERS

1/4 teaspoon	=	1.25	milliliters
1/2 teaspoon	=	2.5	milliliters
3/4 teaspoon	=	3.75	milliliters
1 teaspoon	=	5.0	milliliters
1-1/4 teaspoons	=	6.25	milliliters
1-1/2 teaspoons	=	7.5	milliliters
1-3/4 teaspoons	=	8.75	milliliters
2 teaspoons	=	10.0	milliliters
1 tablespoon	=	15.0	milliliters
2 tablespoons	=	30.0	milliliters

FAHRENHEIT TO CELSUIS

F		C
200 - 205	=	95
220 - 225	=	105
245 - 250	=	120
275	=	135
300 - 305	=	150
325 - 330	=	165
345 - 350	=	175
370 - 375	=	190
400 - 405	=	205
425 - 430	=	220
445 - 450	=	230
470 - 475	=	245
500	=	260

The metric system is based on units of 10. The multiples of 10 are always designated by the same prefix regardless of the base unit specified. Some commonly used prefixes include:

Kilo - 1000
deci - 0.1
centi - 0.01
milli - 0.001

1 meter is about 3 inches longer than a yard

100 grams (of cheese for instance) is about 3-1/2 oz.

Zero degrees Celsius is 32 degrees Fahrenheit, 100 degrees Celsius is 212 degrees Fahrenheit

NOTES:

NOTES: